100 APPLIQUÉ MOTIFS

100
APPLIQUÉ
MOTIFS

Deborah "Ismoyo" Green

 **krause publications**
An imprint of F+W Publications, Inc.

www.mycraftivity.com
Connect. Create. Explore.

A QUARTO BOOK

First published in North America in 2008
By Krause Publications
an imprint of F+W Publications
700 East State Street
Iola, WI 54990-0001
888.459.2873
www.krausebooks.com

ISBN-10 0-89689-725-7
ISBN-13 978-0-8968-9725-0

QUAR.AMO

Conceived, designed, and produced by
Quarto Publishing plc
The Old Brewery
6 Blundell Street
London N7 9BH

Project Editors Rachel Mills and
          Chloe Todd Fordham
Art Director Caroline Guest
Designer Michelle Canatella
Photographers Martin Norris and Phil Wilkins
Copy Editor Betsy Hosegood
Proofreader Diana Chambers
Indexer Diana LeCore

Creative Director Moira Clinch
Publisher Paul Carslake

Color separation by PICA Digital Pte Ltd,
Singapore
Printed in Singapore by Star Standard Industries
(PTE) Ltd

10 9 8 7 6 5 4 3 2 1

CONTENTS

FOREWORD

For years, appliqué has had a kind of old-fashioned ring to it, but nowadays the technique—which consists quite simply of cutting a shape from one fabric and stitching it to another—is experiencing a revival. The craft has been practiced throughout history: early examples have been found in ancient Egyptian tombs, and in the U.S. and Europe appliquéing has long been part of the quilting tradition, as well as serving a practical function in mending torn pieces of clothing. Now, with the boom of modern young women rediscovering old crafts, quilting, knitting, and crocheting are accruing new interest—appliqué is the next thing to get a fresh new look.

A passion for sewing and a love of beautiful fabrics was my starting point. I love discovering how a single color on an appliqué motif gives it one look, while a piece of multicolored printed fabric can give that same motif an entirely different feel. I give tips and techniques in this book, but I'm not one for telling how appliqué is supposed to be done. As with many sewing techniques, there are no hard-and-fast rules.

ABOUT THIS BOOK

This book is organized into four sections, the largest being the "Design and pattern directory" which features over 100 easy-to-make appliqué designs. Browse the directory starting on page 52—or use the neat "Motif selector" on pages 8–11—to locate a motif you like, then follow the simple step-by-step instruction in the "Appliqué tips and techniques" chapter to apply this design to the project of your choice.

TOOLS & MATERIALS (PAGES 12–19)

From choosing materials to buying embellishments and fabric glues, discover all you need to build a collection of materials for all kinds of appliqué.

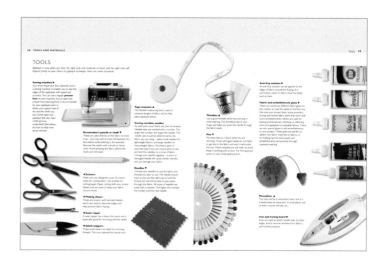

APPLIQUÉ TIPS & TECHNIQUES (PAGES 20–51)

Six major appliqué techniques are demonstrated in this section, complete with step-by-step photography and full written instructions.

Easy to follow step-by-step instructions guide you along the way.

Relevant asides point you in the right direction, offer tips, and suggest alternate methods of practice.

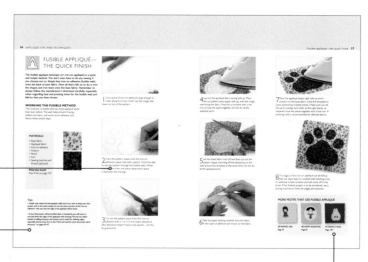

This panel refers you to more motifs from the directory that use this particular technique.

My appliqué wall helped me to organize the selection for this book.

Use this book and the methods described to develop your own style, varying it to suit your personal preference, inspire your own project ideas, and make full use of the materials you have in your stash. From easy, one piece motifs, to multi-piece, dimensional projects, you're sure to find something to fit your skill and interest level.

I hope you will enjoy this book as much as I enjoyed putting it all together.

deborah 'ismoyo' green

ICON SELECTOR

The techniques used in the directory samples are identified with one or more of the following icons.

Hand stitched

Machine stitched

3D appliqué

Freezer paper appliqué

Fusible appliqué

Layered appliqué

Raw edge appliqué

Reverse appliqué

THE DESIGN & PATTERN DIRECTORY (PAGES 52–115)

103 different motif designs are displayed in this section, clearly set out with fabric swatches, method notes, and templates.

This icon specifies the appliqué methods used in the design and refers you to the relevant technique page from Chapter 2.

Additional materials, such as embellishments and decorative stitches, are described here.

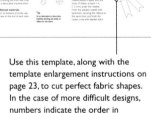

Use this template, along with the template enlargement instructions on page 23, to cut perfect fabric shapes. In the case of more difficult designs, numbers indicate the order in which you should lay out the fabric.

You'll find these panels throughout the directory. They will encourage you to mix and match different motif designs to enhance your project ideas.

PROJECTS (PAGES 116–125)

This chapter will inspire you to create and develop your own appliqué projects. From journals to wall hangings via shoes, hats, clutches, and tops, apply your favorite motif designs to all sorts of accessories and home accents.

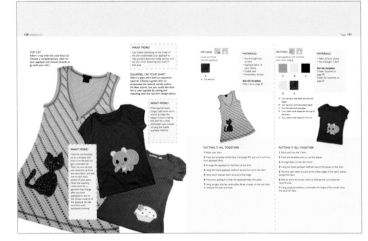

MOTIF SELECTOR

Use the tiles below to select an appliqué design you like, then turn to the relevant page for detailed instruction on how to cut, stitch, and finish your chosen motif.

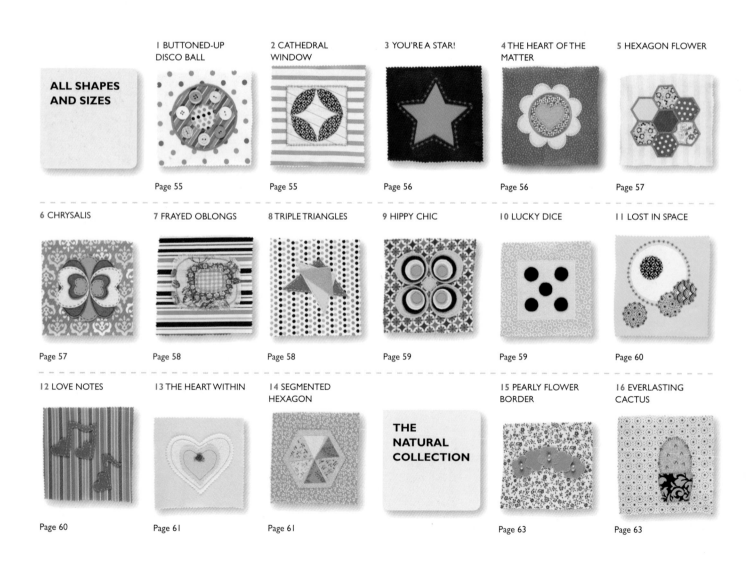

ALL SHAPES AND SIZES

1 BUTTONED-UP DISCO BALL
Page 55

2 CATHEDRAL WINDOW
Page 55

3 YOU'RE A STAR!
Page 56

4 THE HEART OF THE MATTER
Page 56

5 HEXAGON FLOWER
Page 57

6 CHRYSALIS
Page 57

7 FRAYED OBLONGS
Page 58

8 TRIPLE TRIANGLES
Page 58

9 HIPPY CHIC
Page 59

10 LUCKY DICE
Page 59

11 LOST IN SPACE
Page 60

12 LOVE NOTES
Page 60

13 THE HEART WITHIN
Page 61

14 SEGMENTED HEXAGON
Page 61

THE NATURAL COLLECTION

15 PEARLY FLOWER BORDER
Page 63

16 EVERLASTING CACTUS
Page 63

17 WHITE HIBISCUS

Page 64

18 FIVE-LEAVED DAISY

Page 64

19 TULIPS IN BLOOM

Page 65

20 PINK MUSHROOMS

Page 66

21 DREAMY CLOUDS

Page 66

22 FALLING RAINDROPS

Page 67

23 SNACKS FOR SQUIRRELS

Page 67

24 BUTTON TREE

Page 68

25 SCRAP FOREST TREE

Page 68

26 WOODLAND MAPLE

Page 69

27 WATER LILIES IN WINTER

Page 69

28 SPRING CROCUS

Page 70

29 FLOWERS OF FALL

Page 70

30 EVERGREEN FLOWER

Page 71

31 GEOMETRIC FLOWER

Page 72

32 FLORAL ROSETTE

Page 72

33 DAZZLING RIBBON FLOWERS

Page 73

BOYS AND GIRLS COME OUT TO PLAY

34 WAVING BOY

Page 75

35 WAVING GIRL

Page 75

36 PRETTY RED DRESS

Page 76

37 BASEBALL BUDDY

Page 76

38 DANCING WITH BUTTERFLIES

Page 77

39 WATCHING OVER ME

Page 78

40 TIME FOR WORK

Page 78

41 POSH AND PRETTY

Page 79

42 PRECIOUS ANGEL

Page 79

43 STRAWBERRY CLUTCH

Page 80

44 RAIN OR SHINE

Page 80

45 SLEEPING BEAUTY

Page 81

75 CHEEKY SQUIRREL

Page 98

76 LITTLE TAWNY OWL

Page 99

77 QUICK CHICKS

Page 100

78 PUDGY PENGUIN

Page 100

79 SLEEPY TEDDY

Page 101

80 LONG-NECKED GIRAFFE

Page 102

81 SLEEPY TURTLE

Page 102

82 PAW PRINT

Page 103

ALL THINGS GOOD TO EAT AND DRINK

83 JUICY FRUIT

Page 105

84 POLKADOT POPSICLE

Page 105

85 SET THE TABLE

Page 106

86 BIRTHDAY TREAT

Page 106

87 SUSHI SNACK

Page 107

88 SWEET CANDY TREAT

Page 107

89 BUTTON BERRY

Page 108

90 AN APPLE A DAY

Page 108

91 PERFECT PEAR

Page 109

92 WATERMELON WEDGE

Page 109

93 CUPCAKE DELIGHT

Page 110

94 SWEET TOOTH

Page 110

95 COTTON CANDY

Page 111

96 ICE CREAM DREAM

Page 111

97 TWICE AS NICE

Page 112

98 TIME FOR TEA

Page 112

99 PATTERNED TEACUP

Page 113

100 SHAKEN NOT STIRRED

Page 113

101 TASTY TOAST

Page 114

102 SUNNY SIDE UP

Page 114

103 IN YOUR DREAMS

Page 115

CHAPTER ONE

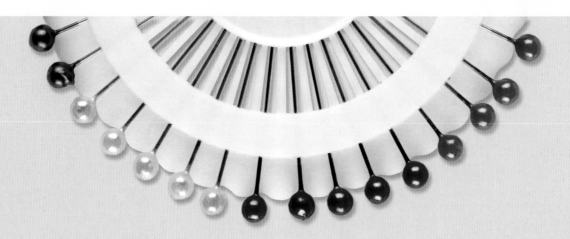

Before you begin making your appliqué designs, you will need to make sure you have the correct tools and materials. This is your guide to locating, buying, and maintaining your unique stash of appliqué essentials.

TOOLS & MATERIALS

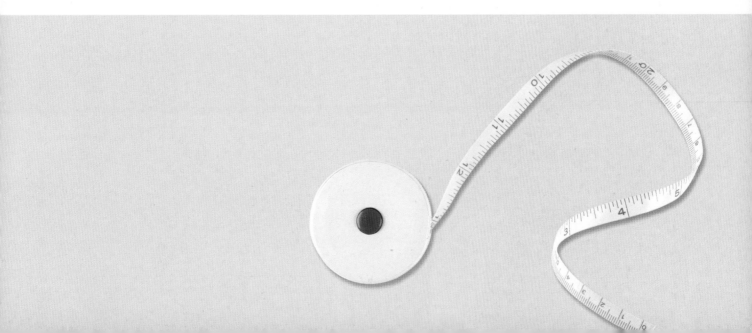

TOOLS

Appliqué is easy when you have the right tools and materials to hand, and the right tools will depend partly on your choice of appliqué technique. Here are some essentials.

Sewing machine ▶

Your most important (but optional) tool is a sewing machine. It enables you to sew the edges of the appliqués with speed and accuracy. You can use a regular **presser foot** on your machine, but an open-toe presser foot (darning foot) is recommended for your appliqué work. It allows you a good view of the stitches while you sew. Some open-toe appliqué feet also have a little groove underneath that allows the foot to slide over dense stitches.

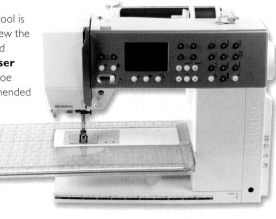

Tape measure ▲

This flexible measuring tool is used to measure lengths of fabric and to help place appliqué pieces.

Sewing machine needles

As with every tool, there are a lot of varieties. Needle sizes are marked with a number. The larger the number, the larger the needle. The needle size should be determined by the fabric you are using—select small needles for lightweight fabrics, and large needles for heavyweight fabrics. Purchase a pack of assorted sizes if you are unsure what to use, and test the needles on a scrap of fabric. Change your needle regularly—a worn or damaged needle will cause uneven stitches and can damage your fabric.

Dressmaker's pencils or chalk ▼

These are used directly on the fabric to mark it up—you may wish to mark the features of a face before embroidering it, for example. Remove the marks with a brush or damp cloth. Avoid pressing the fabric before the marks are removed.

Needles ▼

Choose your needles to suit the fabric and threads you plan to use. The needle should have an eye just the right size to hold the thread, but will still be able to pass easily through the fabric. All types of needles are sized with a number. The higher this number, the smaller and finer the needle.

◀ Scissors

Make sure you designate a pair of scissors solely for cutting fabric. Use another for cutting paper. Paper cutting dulls your scissor blades and you want to keep your fabric scissors sharp.

◀ Pinking shears

These are scissors with serrated blades, which are used to decorate edges and help prevent fabric fraying.

◀ Seam ripper

A seam ripper has a sharp, thin point and is especially good for removing stitches neatly.

◀ Stitch snippers

These small shears are ideal for trimming threads. This is an optional but handy tool.

Anti-fray solution ▶

An anti-fray solution can be applied to the edges of fabrics to prevent fraying. It is particularly useful on fabrics that fray badly, such as linen.

Fabric and embellishment glues ▶

There are numerous different fabric glues on the market, so read the labels to find the one that suits your project best: some provide a strong, permanent fabric bond that works to secure embellishments; others are used for basting and temporary stitching, or adhering trims and appliqués to washable fabrics. There are also special glues to add embellishments to your project. These glues are perfect to adhere non-fabric materials to fabrics, or for holding hard-to-hold jewels and embellishments permanently through repeated washing.

Thimbles ▲

Use a good thimble while hand sewing or embroidering. The thimble protects your finger and helps you push the needle through the fabric easily.

Pins ▼

Pins keep fabrics in place while you are stitching. Those with glass heads are not likely to get lost in the fabric and won't melt under the iron. Plastic-headed pins will melt, so avoid these if working with an iron. For fine appliqué work, try very small appliqué pins.

Pincushion ▲

This may not be a compulsory item, but it is a handy place to store pins. A small plastic tub or even a saucer will also do.

Iron and ironing board ▶

Irons are used to attach fusible web, to press edges, and to remove wrinkles from fabrics and finished projects.

FABRICS

Choice of fabric is possibly the most important and difficult decision you will make when appliquéing as there are many styles, patterns, fibers, and textures to select from. Ideally, you should choose materials that don't fray easily or stretch out of shape. The "Design and pattern directory" that begins on page 52 demonstrates over 100 different motifs that can be made from fabric scraps.

Look for scraps large enough to cover your design, lay out the pattern on the fabric, and cut the motif shapes, taking into account the direction of the pattern. Before you cut, it is best to wash, dry, and iron the fabrics to avoid problems created by materials that shrink at different rates, or dyes that bleed.

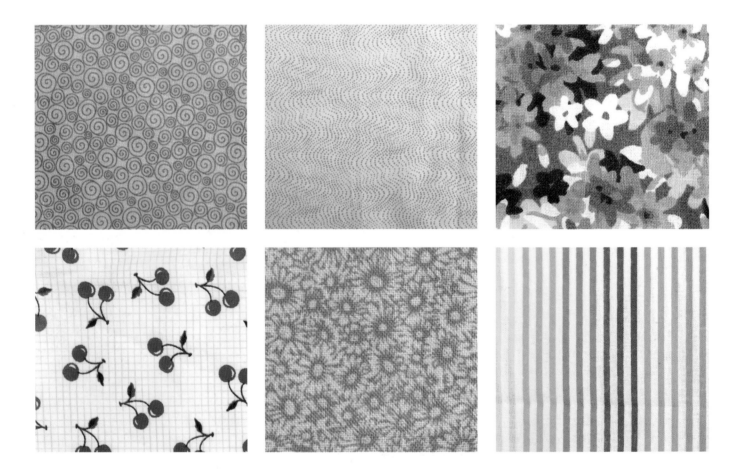

Felts ▶

Felt is different from most other fabrics. It does not fray and pre-washing is unnecessary if you won't be washing your project later. Dependable, sturdy, and easy-to-sew, felt is the perfect material for beginner appliqué artists. Take care, however: felt shrinks substantially when laundered, so if you will be washing your project, pre-washing is a must. Wash the felt by hand in hot water, then rinse in cold, and finally dry. You can use a washing machine for larger pieces, but choose a gentle cycle as wool felt can wrinkle and lose its shape. The more wool in the blend, the more shrinkage will occur.

Cottons ▼

Cotton is a favorite among appliqué artists. Most of the designs in this book are cut from cotton which is easy to sew and does not fray. Use plain or printed cottons like the ones here as your base fabric, and then add fine detail with more unusual materials like silks, gingham, corduroy, and denim, or embellish with some of the ribbon trims sampled on page 19.

OTHER MATERIALS

Once you have chosen your fabrics, you might like to think about stocking up on some useful (though not obligatory) materials like adhesives, batting, and freezer paper. These will assist you greatly when making your appliqués, and encourage you to experiment with more advanced techniques, like dimensional appliqué (see page 34).

Freezer paper

Freezer paper can be very useful for transferring patterns from paper to fabric. Just trace the shape you want to appliqué onto freezer paper and then iron the freezer paper onto your chosen fabric, creating a temporary bond. Now you can cut the fabric. When using this technique, the paper is also used as a guide for stitching (see pages 28–29).

Batting

Batting can be used as an inner layer to give your appliqué dimension. There are many different types of batting on the market, many of which work well for wall hangings and the padded motifs in this book.

Fiberfill

This is traditionally used as a filling for plush animals and pillows. In this book, polyester fiberfill is used in the puffy and stuffed appliqués (see pages 34–35 for details of this technique).

Fusible web (iron-on adhesive)

A good example of this material is *Wonder Under*™, which is used to bond appliqué shapes to the background or base fabric. It comprises a thin layer of adhesive attached to paper backing. When heat is applied, the adhesive melts and sticks to the fabric. Iron *Wonder Under* to the back of a piece of fabric and remove its paper backing to create an iron-on or "easy fuse" appliqué (see pages 26–27).

Interfacing and stabilizers

To prevent puckering and other problems with dense stitching, the fabric must be stabilized. This is done by adding a piece of stabilizer or interfacing to the fabric. Interfacing is applied to the back of the fabric, enhancing its stiffness and providing support; stabilizers give support to densely stitched areas. Either product can be used for the motifs in this book.

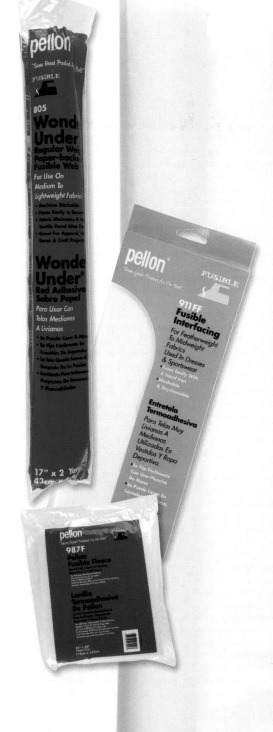

NOTIONS

Many of the motifs presented in the "Design and pattern directory" (pages 52–115) suggest additional materials that will lend character, style, and dimension to you appliqués. You will want to ensure you have plenty of choice, so start your collection now!

Embellishments

There are many, many items that can be used to embellish appliqués. Think of ribbon, cord, fabric flowers, sequins, beads, stick-on gems, and buttons, for example. Use a little, use a lot, use anything that can be sewn or glued on—the possibilities are endless.

The embellishments used in this book are all purchased at local fabric and craft stores to ensure consistency of design. However, you should be encouraged to make your finished projects more personal by using embellishments from your own collection.

Get kitted out ▲
Make sure your stash is well-replenished with ribbon-bows, sparkly gems, and googly eyes.

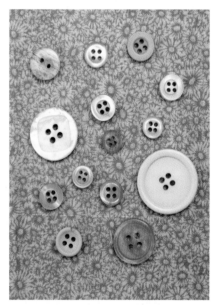

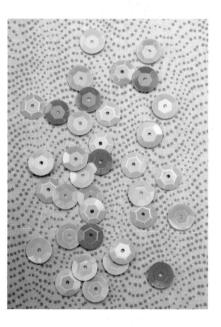

Gemstones ▲
Choose shiny buttons and gemstones to add dimension and sophistication to your designs.

Button-up ▲
A simple button or cluster of sequins will create texture and color, so keep your eye out for loose supplies.

Ribbon trims ▶
Stylish ribbon trims can be used to frame simple compositions, and will look great on any appliqué you intend to give as a gift.

Beads ▲
A well placed bead here and there can transform a design. Make sure you keep some in your reserve stash!

Machine embroidered ribbon trim

Elastic zigzag trim

Embroidered lace

Decorative pleated ribbon trim

Narrow cotton ribbon

Wide silk ribbon

Broderie anglaise

Ribbon reel ▶
To maintain consistency across designs, you may wish to purchase a ribbon reel.

Threads ▼
You may wish to embellish your finished design with decorative stitching (see pages 40–47). Choose a thread color that contrasts with the fabric. Thicker machine embroidery threads, rayons, and metallics can create a beautiful effect. If, however, you want a subtle effect, match the thread color to the fabric—these invisible threads are perfect for machine blind stitching.

Sew in contrasting colors like pink and green...

...red and yellow...

...and purple and orange.

Embroidery floss
Embroidery floss is available in skeins with six strands of embroidery threads loosely wound together. The more strands you use in your needle, the thicker the stitch will be.

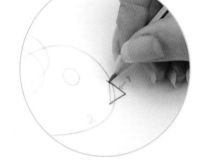

CHAPTER TWO

This chapter is your guide to a number of different appliqué techniques. Try them all or pick your personal favorite. Every technique has step-by-step instructions, clear photos, and additional tips to make your journey through the motifs in this book an easy one. Experiment to find what works best for you.

APPLIQUÉ TIPS & TECHNIQUES

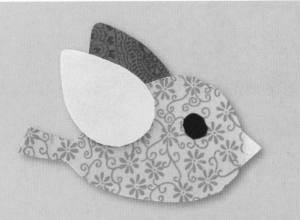

MAKING APPLIQUÉ TEMPLATES

Once you have chosen a motif you like from the directory starting on page 52, take a close look at the accompanying illustrated template. Before using the template it will have to be enlarged to the desired final size and there are various different ways of doing this: you can manually trace the template and photocopy it, or draw a grid to enlarge it, or you can use a scanner and printer to get larger copies. The method you choose will be dependent on the tools you have at your disposal and your personal preference.

TRACING AND PHOTOCOPYING

This is a simple but effective method of copying a template. You will require tracing paper, a pencil, and access to a photocopier machine.

Using tracing paper, trace the template from the motif of your choice. Put this through a copy machine and enlarge it to the desired size. If you don't have access to a copier, you can use the grid method (see page 23) to enlarge your traced image manually.

MATERIALS

- Paper
- Tracing paper
- Pencil
- Photocopier
- Sharp scissors

SCANNING

If you have a computer and scanner, this is the most convenient method of copying a template and it enables you to store the templates electronically.

Scan the template into a computer and enlarge it to the desired size. Make as many prints of each appliqué design as there are overlapping parts in the design. Cut out each printed shape. Where one shape lays over another, cut the top shape from one copy and the bottom shape from another copy.

Tip

Try storing your templates in blank envelopes, using the master template to draw the pattern on the front to indicate what's inside.

MATERIALS

- Scanner
- Computer
- Printer
- Sharp scissors

ENLARGING TEMPLATES USING A GRID

This is the traditional method of enlarging a design. It is more time-consuming and can be less accurate than the other techniques, but it doesn't require any special materials.

1 Use a ruler to make small pencil marks every ½ in. (1.3 cm) along the top and bottom edges of the picture. Connect each mark at the top with the opposite mark at the bottom. Do the same with marks on each side and you will end up with a pattern in a grid.

2 Calculate how much larger you want your final template to be and how large you need to make the squares on a new grid. If you want to double the picture size, draw a second grid with 1 in. (2.6 cm) squares. Copy the picture from the first grid, square by square, drawing the pattern carefully onto your new grid. When you are ready, cut out the pieces. For overlapping pieces, trace all the pieces first, then cut them out.

MATERIALS

- Paper
- Ruler
- Pencil
- Sharp scissors

MAKING MULTI-USE TEMPLATES

If you will be making several appliqués from the same design, you will want them to last. Templates can be used multiple times when they are cut from card stock rather than paper.

1 Begin by drawing and cutting a paper template, enlarging it (if necessary) to the desired size.

2 Use standard paper glue, such as a glue stick, to attach all template parts to a piece of heavy card stock.

3 Once the glue has dried, cut out the templates around the edges with sharp paper scissors.

MATERIALS

- Paper
- Card
- Pencil
- Paper glue
- Sharp scissors

LAYERED APPLIQUÉ

A large number of the motifs in this collection require more than one template, and patterned fabric pieces that overlap in the finished design will need some extra attention. Always start by taking a very close look at the motif: multiple pieces should be cut and applied in a well thought out, logical order. Upfront planning will make your appliquéing a lot easier!

WORKING LAYERED APPLIQUÉ
This is an example of how to appliqué a typical motif with several overlapping pieces. Follow these steps and apply the same process to your own designs.

MATERIALS
- Appliqué fabric(s)
- Base fabric
- Scissors
- Sewing machine and thread
- Tracing paper
- Plain white paper
- Pencil

Find the motif
Bird Garden on page 103

Tip
Have a color plan for your appliqué motif. Start with the base fabric and then select colors that complement it—choose pink tones, earth tones, forest greens, or bright colors, for example.

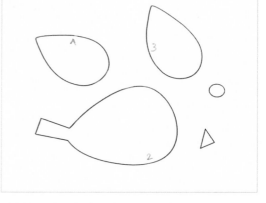

1 Take a close look at the pattern pieces and number them in the order in which the pieces will be put together. Start low and work your way to the top. Find the undermost layer and mark it number 1. Proceed up to the uppermost layer.

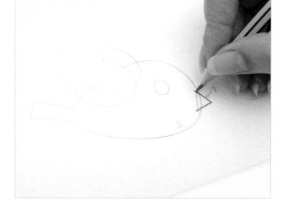

2 Trace the pieces one by one, copying the numbers too. To be sure that no gaps appear in your final design, draw the lower parts slightly larger, especially where they are overlapped by upper parts: there is no need to sew the edges that will be hidden when the appliqué is complete. By numbering the appliqué pieces, you can tell which edges will be covered by another piece.

MORE MOTIFS THAT USE LAYERED APPLIQUÉ

32 FLORAL ROSETTE
Page 72

67 WIDE-EYED OWL
Page 94

91 PERFECT PEAR
Page 109

The layered appliqué icon has not been applied to the directory samples. Unless stated otherwise, it is used in all the designs in the directory. Above you'll find some great examples to get you started.

3 For multi-layer appliqués that feature small parts entirely on top of larger parts, lay out the components as you please, and attach the smaller piece(s) to the larger one(s). When done, treat the joined layers as a single appliqué.

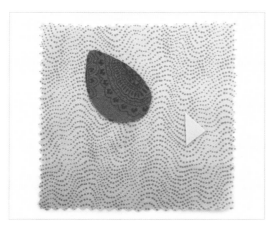

4 Position and appliqué layer one: the pieces that don't overlap any other parts. Always work on the lowest layer first.

5 After the first layer is appliquéd, position the next layer and repeat until the design is finished.

FUSIBLE APPLIQUÉ— THE QUICK FINISH

The fusible appliqué technique (or iron-on appliqué) is a quick and simple method. You don't even have to do any sewing if you choose not to: Simply fuse iron-on adhesive (fusible web) onto the back of your fabric. Now all that's left to to do is trim the shapes and iron them onto the base fabric. Remember to always follow the manufacturer's directions carefully, especially when regarding heat and pressing times for the fusible web and fabrics that you have chosen.

WORKING THE FUSIBLE METHOD

The invention of fusible web has made appliqué easier than ever before. The web helps prevent fraying, stiffens the fabric, and works as an adhesive. Just follow these simple steps.

MATERIALS

- Base fabric
- Appliqué fabric
- Iron-on adhesive
- Scissors
- Pencil
- Iron
- Sewing machine and thread (optional)

Find the motif
Paw Print on page 103

Tips

• Fusible web makes the final appliqué stiffer, but if you wish to keep your final project soft to the touch, simply cut out the center portion of the iron-on adhesive—this way only the edge of the appliqué will be fused.

• If your final project will be handled often or laundered, you will want to securely finish the edges of the appliqués with stitching. This has the added benefit of adding character and texture, and is useful for defining edges, especially internal ones. Turn to the "Hand and machine sewn decorative stitch directory" on pages 40–47.

1 Cut a piece of iron-on adhesive large enough to cover all parts of your motif. Lay this rough side down on top of the pattern.

2 Trace the pattern shape onto the iron-on adhesive's paper side with a pencil. (You'll be able to see the pattern through the fusible web.) When tracing more than one piece, leave extra space in-between the tracings.

3 Cut out the pattern piece from the iron-on adhesive with a ½ in. (13 mm) seam allowance (this allowance doesn't have to be specific—do this by guesswork).

4 Lay out the appliqué fabric wrong side up. Place the cut pattern piece paper side up, with the rough side facing the fabric. Press for a moment with a hot iron to fuse the layers together. Do this for all the appliqué parts.

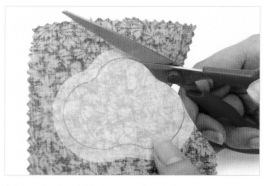

5 Let the fused fabric cool off and then cut out the pattern shape, trimming off the allowance on the web around the template at the same time. Do this for all the appliqué parts.

6 Peel the paper backing carefully from the fabric. A thin layer of adhesive will remain on the fabric.

7 Place the appliqué shape right side up and in position on the base fabric. (Use the template to assist positioning multiple pieces.) Make sure you let the parts overlap each other at the right places, as required. Fuse the pieces together with a hot iron. A pressing cloth is recommended for delicate fabrics.

8 The edges of the iron-on appliqué can be left as they are (easy fuse) or covered with stitching. Iron-on adhesive is heat sensitive and will come off in the dryer. If the finished project is to be laundered, use a sewing machine to finish the edges permanently.

MORE MOTIFS THAT USE FUSIBLE APPLIQUÉ

35 WAVING GIRL
Page 75

46 HAPPY VALENTINE
Page 81

91 PERFECT PEAR
Page 109

FREEZER PAPER APPLIQUÉ

This technique uses freezer paper as a guide for stitching. Freezer paper, which can be purchased at grocery or craft stores, is shiny and waxy on one side (the sticky side) and matte on the other. Commonly used in appliqué, freezer paper is ironed onto fabric to form a bond, and is easily removed afterwards. This method is most often used in combination with blind hem stitch, the most invisible of all appliqué machine stitches, which resembles the classic needle turn.

WORKING THE FREEZER PAPER METHOD

This traditional method of appliqué is ideal for more complex shapes or for areas where you don't want the fabric edges to show. Stitching can be worked by hand, if preferred.

MATERIALS

- Appliqué fabric
- Base fabric
- Freezer paper
- Pencil
- Scissors
- Iron
- Tweezers
- Thread to match the color of your appliqué fabric
- Sewing machine

Find the motif
Perfect Pear on page 109

MORE MOTIFS THAT USE FREEZER PAPER APPLIQUÉ

45 SLEEPING BEAUTY
Page 81

59 BUMBLING ALONG
Page 90

1 Copy the pattern onto the freezer paper. It is easiest to draw on the dull side, but if you are having a hard time tracing through the freezer paper, use a lightbox or hold your work up to a window.

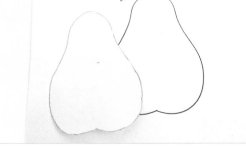

2 Cut out the shape without adding a seam allowance.

3 Iron the freezer paper shape, shiny side down, onto the wrong side of the appliqué fabric. Don't use a steam setting on your iron; a brief pressing is enough to adhere the freezer paper to the fabric.

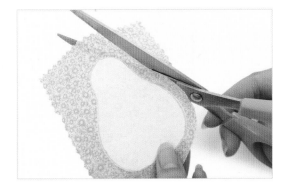

4 Once the freezer paper has bonded to the fabric, cut out the fabric, leaving a seam allowance of approximately ½ in. (13 mm).

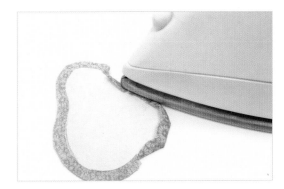

5 Fold the seam allowance straight down over the paper template and press. Clip corners and curves to ease the turning of the fabric. Get close to the paper, but be careful you don't cut through it.

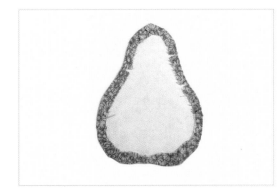

6 Fold the seam allowance down around the entire shape. If you don't need the paper as a stitching guide, you can remove it now. Otherwise keep it in, as shown here.

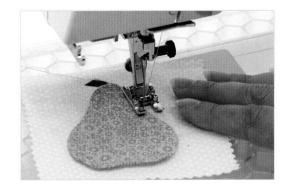

7 Set up your sewing machine for a blind hem stitch. Use a thread color that matches the appliqué shape. The stitch width should be just wide enough to catch a few threads beyond the folded edge of your appliqué piece. The machine should make several straight stitches in the base fabric next to the appliqué piece, and then zigzag one stitch into the appliqué fabric. Don't complete the stitching until you have read step 8.

8 Turn the appliqué right side up and place it on the base fabric. To remove the paper, appliqué around your motif until you are about 1 in. (2.5 cm) from the closing. Use tweezers to pull the paper out through the opening and then finish your stitching. With larger pieces, it's often easier to turn your work over and make a small slash behind the appliqué. The freezer paper will help prevent the scissors going through the actual design, but take care: remove the paper through the slash slowly and gently.

RAW EDGE APPLIQUÉ

The raw edge technique is the easiest and fastest appliqué technique and adds a fun and casual look to your projects—sometimes, a rough edge is exactly what you're looking for! The shapes are cut out (with or without pinking shears) and sewn to the base fabric, but the seams are left on show. If you want to use the raw edge technique but don't want the edges to unravel, go for a non-fraying fabric like felt, as shown in the step-by-step sequence.

WORKING THE RAW EDGE METHOD

This method involves stitching just inside the raw edge of the shape and allowing the fabric edge to fray naturally. How much of an edge you leave depends on the effect you want.

MATERIALS

- Fabrics
- Threads
- Pins
- Sewing machine (optional)
- Pinking shears (optional)

Find the motif
Pink Mushrooms on page 66

Tip

If you don't want the fabric to unravel, make sure that fabrics that fray are stabilized before using the raw edge appliqué method. Either fuse a layer of interfacing to the back of the fabric, or apply an anti-fray solution to the edges. Alternatively, finish the appliqué by sewing satin stitch on the raw edges instead of straight stitch inside.

The Right Foot

A special blind stitch presser foot comes in handy for machine blind hem stitch. It has a special edge to guide your stitching and makes sure the diagonal stitches go to the right place. Most sewing machines that have a blind hem stitch come with a blind stitch presser foot that will look like the one above.

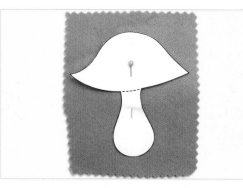

1 Pin the template onto your appliqué fabric. This mushroom motif, from page 66, is going to be cut as one piece for simplicity.

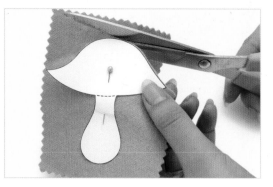

2 Cut out the motif without seam allowances. For added character you can use pinking shears.

MORE MOTIFS THAT USE RAW EDGE APPLIQUÉ

9 HIPPY CHIC
Page 59

13 THE HEART WITHIN
Page 61

29 FLOWERS OF FALL
Page 70

37 BASEBALL BUDDY
Page 76

60 MADAME
BUTTERFLY
Page 90

75 CHEEKY SQUIRREL
Page 98

3 Place the appliqué motif on your base fabric and pin it in place, keeping the pin(s) well out of the way of the edges, as far as possible.

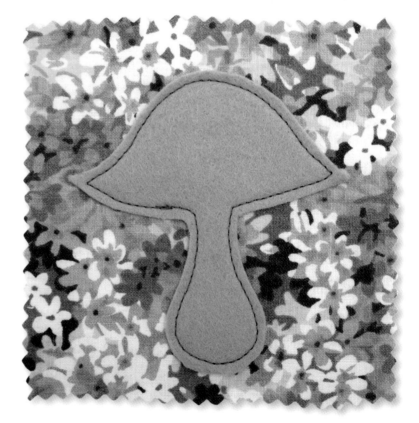

4 Stitch a straight stitch inside the edge of the appliqué using your sewing machine or by hand. Straight stitch will encourage the frayed edges; when the project is laundered, the raw edge will fray, but the stitching will stop it fraying too far.

REVERSE APPLIQUÉ

Create interesting results using this intriguing technique, which involves removing fabric rather than adding it. Cut away the design from the base fabric, allowing the backing or lining fabric to show through the cut-out shape. If desired, the backing fabric can be made from two or more fabrics that have been seamed together, creating an even more exciting result. Use reverse appliqué on its own, or combine it with one or more of the other appliqué methods, for a truly multilayered look.

The appliqué fabric will be placed under the base fabric, so it must be cut large enough to cover the final shape, plus a good seam allowance.

WORKING THE REVERSE METHOD

This technique involves adding layers beneath the base fabric rather than above it. The example shows just one backing layer but you can cut through this too and add another layer behind that one, if desired.

MATERIALS

- Appliqué fabric
- Base fabric
- Pins
- Marker pencil
- Scissors
- Threads
- Basting glue

Find the motif
You're a Star! on page 56

2 Position the appliqué template on top of the base fabric and pin it in place.

3 Mark the pattern on the base fabric using a fabric marker pencil (make sure that the marks can be easily removed afterward). Cut away the inside of the design.

4 Dab a few dots of basting glue around the cut-out edge on the back of the base fabric. Place the appliqué fabric behind the hole. Be sure both fabrics are right side up.

MORE MOTIFS THAT USE REVERSE APPLIQUÉ

74 REVERSE BABY ELEPHANT Page 98   **61 LOVELY LADYBUG** Page 91   **27 WATER LILLIES IN WINTER** Page 69

5 Start to sew a (decorative) stitch around the edge of the top piece to secure the layers. For more information on choosing a stitch, see the tip below.

Tip

The choice of finishing stitches depends on the desired final look and the type of fabric used. With non-fraying base fabrics, go for any decorative stitch. Work it around the edge, as in the example here. If the base fabric frays easily, choose a satin stitch (page 43) and sew over the raw edge to enclose it.

6 When using a stitch with a distinct design, like the one shown here, aim to match it around repeat areas, such as the points of this star, and try to make the join as inconspicuous as possible.

DIMENSIONAL APPLIQUÉ

Adding three-dimensional techniques to your appliqué can make your project even more interesting, especially if you combine flat methods of appliqué with selective dimensional appliqué, as in the examples shown here. There are several ways of adding depth and dimension to your work. The techniques here use fiberfill or batting to make the pieces puffy, padded, or stuffed, but there are other methods too, such as fabric folding, outlined on pages 36–37.

PUFFY APPLIQUÉ ▼

A puffy appliqué lies on top of the base fabric. Dimension is added by filling two pieces of fabrics sewn together with fiberfill. This technique is explained step by step on the opposite page.

PADDED APPLIQUÉ ▲

Padded appliqué is where a batting material, such as the cotton or fiberfill commonly used in quilts, is sandwiched either between the appliqué material and the base fabric, or on the entire back of the base fabric. If you only sandwich the batting between the appliqué and the base fabric, cut the batting slightly smaller than the actual template, glue it in place, and appliqué around the whole fabric element. This motif, found on page 82, uses padded appliqué on the ribbon and kimono designs.

Tip

Never final press your dimensional appliqué as this could flatten it. If the fabric is creased you may find that steaming smoothes it out.

STUFFED APPLIQUÉ ▶

This is an easy way of adding dimension. When stitching around your appliqué piece, leave an opening before you reach the end. Push a small amount of fiberfill in under the shape and finish your stitching to close the gap. This motif appears on page 89.

CREATING PUFFY APPLIQUÉ

This is a good way to add dimension to a select area of your design. Simply cut your shape twice, join the pieces, and stuff, before attaching to the base fabric.

MATERIALS

- Appliqué fabric
- Scissors
- Sewing machine
- Fiberfill
- Needle and thread

Find the motif
Sunny Side Up on page 114

MORE MOTIFS THAT USE 3D APPLIQUÉ

17 WHITE HIBISCUS
Page 58

98 TIME FOR TEA
Page 106

1 Cut two pieces of the same fabric for the "puffy" part of your project instead of one, adding a ½ in. (13 mm) seam allowance to your template.

2 Sew both parts together with wrong sides facing, stopping before stitching is complete. Stuff the form with fiberfill until the desired fullness is achieved. If the appliqué is small, use a pencil to push the filling inside.

3 Finish stitching the two pieces of fabric closed.

4 Place the puffy appliqué on your base fabric, turn the project over, and hand sew—through both the base fabric and the center of the puffy appliqué—to attach the shape.

5 Turn the fabric back over and check that the appliqué is firmly attached.

THREE-DIMENSIONAL FABRIC FOLDING

A simple way of adding dimension to your appliqué is simply to fold your fabrics to make loose standing appliqué pieces. The thicker and stiffer your fabric, the more obvious this effect will be, so this is a good way of using up scraps of thick dressmaking or upholstery fabrics that you might otherwise consider to be too heavy for appliqué techniques. Because the back of the pieces may be seen, you can create double-sided pieces by fusing two pieces together. This will also help to thicken and stiffen medium-weight fabrics like cotton, which is used for the rabbit ears shown below.

Find the motif
Funny Bunny
on page 97
White Hibiscus
on page 64

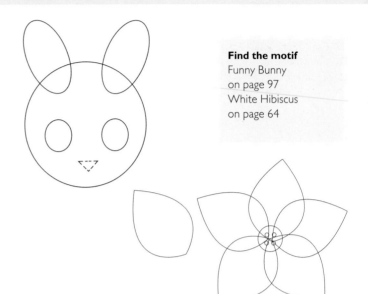

These bunny ears work brilliantly with this technique—they have just enough dimension to draw your attention but don't look out of place on the otherwise flat appliqué. The wobbly eyes add another humorous three-dimensional element. The steps needed to create this appliqué are shown opposite.

Adding dimension to leaves is easy. Cut out the leaf shape from your chosen appliqué fabric and fold it in half, pressing down firmly to create a neat groove along which to sew. Now, lay the leaf on your base fabric and sew a straight stitch right down the middle along the fold.

Tip
Heavyweight fabrics and felts are best used for folding fabrics. If you wish to fold lighter-weight fabrics like cotton, iron fusible web onto the back to stiffen it.

Tip
Instead of folding each leaf, fold each petal for a three-dimensional flower. See Spring Crocus on page 70.

MAKING FOLDED APPLIQUÉ

Folded appliqué gives your design that little extra detailing that makes it stand out from the ordinary. These instructions are for rabbit ears, but the same principles apply for other shapes.

MATERIALS

- Appliqué fabric
- Scissors
- Iron
- Fusible web
- Sewing machine
- Needle and thread

Find the motif
Funny Bunny on page 97

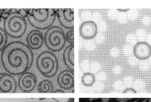

3 Reinforce the edges of the pieces with machine stitch, in this case with zigzag stitch.

4 Fold the bottom part one-third over—for leaves or petals you may wish to fold the whole shape in half. Hand sew the fold securely at the bottom, and the ear is ready to be incorporated into your project.

1 Cut each piece that you want to fold twice—in this case, cut four ears, two for each bunny ear.

2 Iron fusible web to the back of two of the ears. Place a remaining ear on top and then iron to fuse the ear pieces together. You now have two double-sided ears.

5 In this case, the ears are slipped behind the face and caught in the stitching around it. Think about different ways of attaching the shapes you are using.

COLOR AND COMPOSITION

Before you rush out and buy vast quantities of different colored material, it is a good idea to be sure of what you really need. Think of where your appliqué design will be placed. If your final project is to adorn a dress, pick fabrics that complement or contrast with the base fabric. If, on the other hand, you're making an appliqué to embellish a baby gift, try pastel-colored fabrics. Consider color carefully, and don't jump in without a clear end goal. Your work could be in vain if the color scheme doesn't feel right.

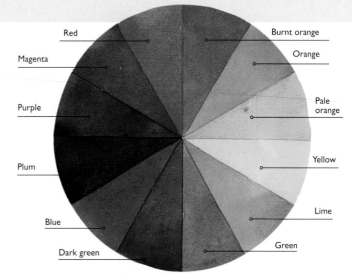

Red
Magenta
Purple
Plum
Blue
Dark green
Burnt orange
Orange
Pale orange
Yellow
Lime
Green

CHOOSING COLORS

Dive into your scrap fabric stash. Choose colors that might suit your project, including prints if you wish. Notice different textures too, as different kinds of fabric will add variety to the overall look.

Decide whether you want all the fabrics to be of a similar value—for example, pastels colors—or whether you prefer a mix of light, medium, and dark colors in your design.

ARRANGING COLORS

Color is a subjective experience. The final color combination should be appealing to you and your target viewer, so play around with your colors before you commit them to your design. You will notice that the "feel" of a motif can change (for better or for worse) by changing the colors. Here's how to begin:

Arrange the fabrics loosely, as you would group them in the appliqué. Take a good look to determine whether any one piece jumps out at you because it is too light or too dark. If so, either remove it, or balance it with a complementary color (see the "Color wheel" above right).

"Complementaries" initialise a dynamic contrast, creating drama and focus in your composition, but take care to apply these colors subtly so as not to overwhelm the composition, or disrupt the color balance.

Tip
Take a trip to the paint section of your local hardware store. You will find hundreds of colors on swatch cards indicating their different hues. Why not use these as "color combining" inspiration?

THE COLOR WHEEL

The color wheel (above) arranges primary and secondary colors in a "rainbow circle" and demonstrates the concepts of "harmonious" and "complementary" colors. Browns, grays, white, and black are found only on very complex models, but you will find this basic color wheel to be an invaluable tool when picking colors for your appliqués.

Harmonious colors
Red, pale magenta, and purple are harmonious colors because they are next-door colors on the wheel. As a general rule, any range of harmonious colors will work well together. Try mixing green, lime, yellow, and orange fabrics, or green, dark green, blue, and plum.

Complementary colors
Orange and blue are opposites on the wheel and create a bright, lively contrast. Red and green, and purple and yellow are also well-partnered. Consider the tonal value of the two colors involved: the closer they are in tone, the more they will "vibrate" visually—a bit like a pop-art painting.

Harmonious colors (with a twist)
Orange, magenta, red, and pale pink are a standard range of harmonious colors; but add a complementary blue to the mix and you will transform the design with a color contrast that gives the pattern definition and character.

Tonal values
Working with light/dark color contrasts is a useful way of pulling out specific shapes. Notice how the doll's hairstyle (left) stands out against the pale cream base fabric. If you want a softer coloring, use a range of tonal values, like a pale pink, mid-tone pink, and dark pink, as illustrated in the angel motif, left.

BUILDING A COMPOSITION

The more you experiment with composition, the more it will seem like second nature. Try things out as you go, and don't be scared or put off if you struggle to get started. Play around with your appliqué on the base fabric: first, place it in the center; then see how it looks if arranged off-center. You will know when you have found a harmonious location as the final "feel" of the design will be well-balanced and pleasing to the eye.

Finding a focus

One-piece appliqués work especially well when they are placed centrally on the base fabric, but there are plenty of neat finishes that will redirect the eye, leading it off-center. Finding an unconventional focus will add an element of surprise or humor to your designs. Try positioning a fabric flower embellishment off-center (above middle), or twist the whole design diagonally to imply an element of flight or movement, as in the bee design (above right).

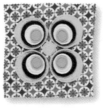

Using repetition

The visual impact of repetition is always arresting, whether it is applied randomly (as in the above center example) or more formally (as in the tulip design, above left). Duplicate any motif and you will create a larger, striking, graphic pattern (above right).

Checking the balance

If you feel there is too much empty space in your design, try adding another element to balance the composition, such as an apple button (above center) or a ribbon trim (above right). However, make sure you give your motif space to breathe; less is more in the above cactus design.

PATTERNED FABRICS

Be cautious when using busy prints. Simple patterns, stripes, and dots are easier to work with than more detailed prints, as are small-scale or "blurry" patterns.

If you apply only one patterned fabric in your design, you will draw attention to this area, so choose wisely. The more patterns you introduce to the project, the more complex and potentially problematic it will be. Use patterned fabrics confidently and with careful consideration of the other elements at work in your design, and you won't go wrong.

Using one plain fabric and one patterned fabric, either as background or motif, will emphasize the motif shape, especially in one-piece appliqués like these leaf variations.

If you plan to use two or more patterned fabrics in your design, choose a uniting theme, such as "spots" (as in the popsicle design, above left). Alternatively, try finding patterns that share the same tonal value, like the soft pastel pinks employed in this flower motif (above right).

Selecting an area

Sometimes a small scrap cut from a large-scale print can provide just the touch of color you need. This leaf, in two shades of green, can be used for its color alone; when used as a small patch, it will no longer be identifiable as a leaf.

Machine stitching is tight, neat, and durable: use if you intend to machine wash your appliqués

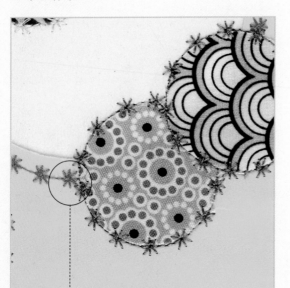

Appliqué stitches serve a very basic practical function: to attach one material or fabric to another. But they can also be used decoratively, adding personality, style, and a certain homespun quality to your design. Deciding whether to hand stitch or machine stitch can be difficult. This is your guide to choosing the right stitch for your appliqué projects.

Hand stitching is looser, and can add personality and spontaneity to your design: use for fine detail and decoration

HAND AND MACHINE SEWN DECORATIVE STITCH DIRECTORY

Once your appliqué motif is designed, you may wish to add fine detail with decorative stitches. The following pages feature six major stitches—zigzag, satin, blanket, running, backstitch, and French knot—in their machine and hand sewn variations where appropriate. Some of these stitches are neat and unassuming, some are elegant, others more flamboyant—peruse these pages to find the technique that best suits your appliqué design.

RUNNING STITCH

Hand embroidered stitches are a great way to finish appliqué motifs if you don't have a sewing machine available, or just want that handmade look—the basic running stitch is a great place to start.

Running stitch can be used practically and decoratively, or in delicate sewing where the stitches will be permanent. Bold, simple, and strong, it creates movement in the above design, which you will find on page 57 of the directory.

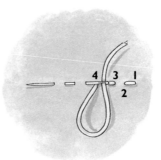

Basic running stitch
Work lines from right to left. Bring needle up at **1**, down at **2**, and up at **3** to begin next repeat at **4**.

The whipped running stitch defines this sleepy turtle's body. You will find this motif on page 102.

Whipped running stitch

Work a line of running stitch. Bring contrast color in a blunt needle up at **I**. Pass needle under each stitch from top to bottom without piercing fabric. Pass needle through to back at center top of last stitch.

MORE MOTIFS THAT USE RUNNING STITCH

37 BASEBALL BUDDY
Page 76

40 TIME FOR WORK
Page 78

Laced running stitch

Work a line of running stitch. Bring contrast color in a blunt needle up at **I**. Pass needle under second stitch from bottom to top, then under next stitch from top to bottom, without piercing fabric. Repeat to end of line. Pass needle through to back at center top or bottom of last stitch.

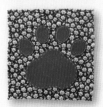

82 PAW PRINT
Page 103

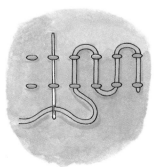

Interlaced running stitch

Work 2 or 3 lines of running stitch with the stitches exactly above each other. With a contrast color and a blunt needle, work as for laced running stitch, passing needle vertically under each group of stitches in turn.

Parallel lines of whipped, laced, and interlaced running stitches can be matched or staggered at different spacings to produce a variety of surface patterns.

Tip

Running stitch combines well with backstitch (see page 44) as both are very simple stitches. Work the stitching in a contrasting color when you want it to stand out, or in a toning color to blend in.

ZIGZAG STITCHING

Zigzag stitch is a good, plain stitch for securing your appliqué pieces and may be used to neaten any raw edges that are liable to fray. It can also be useful as a decorative stitch.

On most machines, both the stitch width and stitch length can be varied, giving you a wide range of zigzag sizes. The heavier the fabric, the larger the zigzag stitches. The low stitch count makes for fast sewing and allows you to appliqué small or detailed shapes. You'll also find that the lighter density of this finishing stitch makes the stitches seem to disappear, so smaller design elements are not overwhelmed.

You may find the hand sewn zigzag stitch a little arduous if you have a sewing machine that can work the stitch more efficiently. But if you have the time, and you are willing to be patient, hand embroidered zigzag will give your appliqués an unmatched authenticity. The basic technique is outlined in the illustration below.

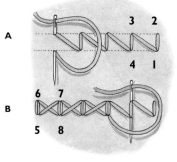

MORE MOTIFS THAT USE ZIGZAG STITCH

17 WHITE HIBISCUS

Page 64

18 FIVE-LEAVED DAISY

Page 64

27 WATER LILIES IN WINTER

Page 69

Basic zigzag stitch

This stitch is worked in two journeys:
A: Work first journey from right to left. Bring needle up at **1**, down at **2**, up at **1**, down at **3**, and up at **4**. Begin next repeat by inserting needle at **3**. Repeat, ending with a vertical stitch at left.
B: Work second journey from left to right. Bring needle up at **5**, down at **6**, up at **5**, down at **7**, and up at **8**. Repeat, doubling each vertical and crossing each sloping stitch.

SATIN STITCHING

Zigzag stitching and satin stitching are the two most popular finishes used in appliqué. While a zigzag stitch will emphasize the edges of your appliqué, a satin stitch will draw attention away from this area, and lead the eye to the center of the fabric or design.

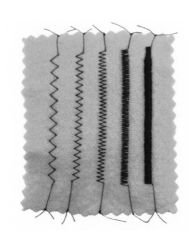

This sample shows the transition from wide zigzag to satin stitch—the difference is in the stitch length. Play around with the stitch length control on your machine until you achieve the desired effect.

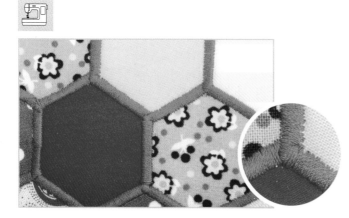

This attractive machine stitch is more closely spaced than its hand sewn variation: it is the most durable of stitches, and boasts a speed impossible to match by hand. The heavy thread outline emphasizes patch shapes but is not well suited to complex or tiny patches.

Hand sewn satin stitches can be used to fill small areas with closely packed stitches, forming a smooth surface. They are suitable for working small motifs, such as flowers, leaves, or facial detail. Cotton or silk floss is the best choice of thread for these stitches and using two or three strands together will give a flat, glossy appearance.

WORKING THE MACHINE SEWN SATIN STITCH

• Start with a stitch length slightly more than zero, then adjust the width according to your preference. If the thread builds up, increase stitch length gradually to get a smooth stitch. If you see zigzag stitches, decrease the length for a more solid line of stitching.

• When you stitch along the patch edge, you want the stitches to cover the raw edge and extend into the background fabric by a thread or two.

• With a good satin stitch, it's all about tension and stitch length. It's very important to keep the tension on your stitches nice and loose. You will know you have the tension right when the needle thread is pulled to the underside and no bobbin thread can be seen on top.

• Use an appliqué foot if your machine has one, and use a stabilizer to obtain even stitches and to help prevent puckering.

• By starting the satin stitch in the center of a line rather than in the corner, it is much easier to match up at the end.

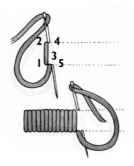

Straight satin stitch

Work from left to right: Bring needle up at **1**, down at **2**, up at **3**, down at **4**, and up at **5**. Repeat as required. Stitches should be close together with no fabric showing between them.

Slanted satin stitch

Choose the direction of the slant to suit the shape: stitches that are too long will not keep their shape. Stitches on different areas may be worked in different directions to catch the light. Begin at center of shape: bring needle up at **1** and down at **2**. The first stitch sets the slant for all subsequent stitches. Work parallel stitches from center out to right. Then return to center and work parallel stitches out to left.

BACKSTITCH

Backstitch is subtle but durable and, like its sister stitch (the running stitch), it is best used to define outline.

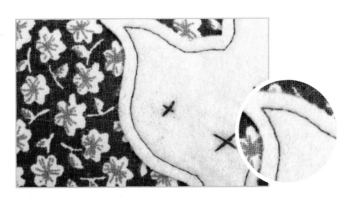

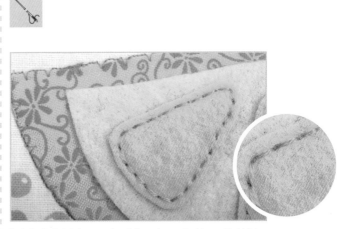

Basic backstitch is best used to define edges, as in this motif which is found on page 105.

The machine sewn equivalent to the hand sewn backstitch is the basic machine-worked straight stitch. As you can see, the two stitches—one hand sewn, one machine sewn—are almost identical. Set to the "straight stitch" function, the machine will produce a basic line of connected stitches, quickly and to great effect. This works especially well when you wish to indicate outline, as in the above example which you will find on page 87.

The hand worked backstitch is looser than the machine worked straight stitch, but it still retains a clean, discreet character. Once you've mastered the basic blanket stitch, experiment with the three variations which are illustrated opposite.

Sewing machines differ, so consult your manual for basic operating procedures and identification of the controls. Choose a needle size and stitch length to suit your fabrics, using the table below:

Fabric	Stitch length	U.S. needle size	European needle size
Lightweight cottons, polycottons, silks	short: 8–10 stitches per inch (2.5–3 mm)	9–11	70–80
Medium-weight linens, twill, light denim, cottons	long: 7–9 stitches per inch (3–3.5 mm)	11–14	80–90

Tip

If you are having trouble threading a needle, try wetting the eye of the needle (not the thread) to thread it more easily. This also works on sewing machine needles. Holding the needle over a piece of white paper will help you see the eye.

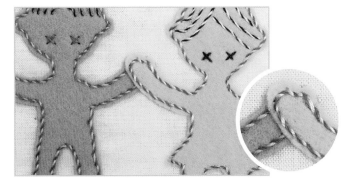

Whipped backstitch can be worked in more than one color. You will find this design on page 85.

MORE MOTIFS THAT USE BACKSTITCH

37 BASEBALL BUDDY
Page 76

57 SMILEY FACE
Page 89

75 CHEEKY SQUIRREL
Page 98

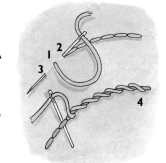

A

B

C

D

Basic backstitch
A: Bring needle up at **1**, down at **2**, and up at **3**. The distance **1–2** should be the same as the distance **1–3**. Begin next stitch by inserting needle at **1**. Repeat as required keeping stitch length constant.

Whipped backstitch
B: Bring contrast color in a blunt needle up at **4**. Pass the needle under each stitch from top to bottom without piercing the fabric. Pass needle to wrong side at center top of last backstitch.

Threaded backstitch
C: This is worked in a similar way to whipped backstitch, but the contrasting color is passed alternately up and down under the backstitches, as in the top diagram.

Double threaded backstitch
D: A second lacing thread may be added in the same way, without catching the loops of the first, as illustrated by the bottom diagram.

BLANKET STITCH

Blanket stitch gives an authentic look to appliqué projects. So if you find the satin stitch too heavy or dominant, consider sewing with blanket. Even worked on the sewing machine, this stitch seems almost hand done—although of course it's a lot faster!

The stitch width and length will depend on what looks best with your fabrics and design motifs. Smaller stitches prevent fraying and are easier when stitching around small or complex shapes. Big patches however, look better with longer and wider stitches, leaving a majority of the raw edge uncovered.

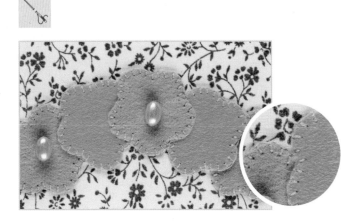

The hand worked blanket stitch is a fairly simple stitch, although it requires some care to get the stitches even. It is a popular and traditional stitch for appliqué and will definitely give your appliqué a handcrafted look.

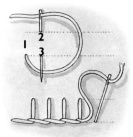

Basic blanket stitch

Working from left to right, the twisted edge forms at the lower line:
Bring needle up at **1**, down at **2**, and up at **3**, with thread looped under needle. Pull through. Take care to tighten the stitches equally throughout for a neat twisted edge. Repeat to the right. Fasten down the last loop by taking a small stitch along the lower line.

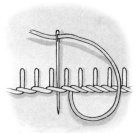

Whipped blanket stitch

Blanket stitch is easily enhanced by whipping the lower edge with a contrasting thread and a blunt needle. Working from right to left, pass needle under lower thread of each blanket stitch from top to bottom as shown, without piercing fabric.

FRENCH KNOT

The French knot is a popular embroidery technique, and is nearly always hand worked. The thread is wound around the needle, as in the illustrations below, and knotted around itself. Large groups of French knots can be used to fill a space. Single, or small groups of French knots can be used to indicate a dot on your design, such as an eye, nose, or decorative element.

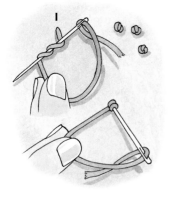

Tip
For a larger knot use heavier thread. Never wind more than twice.

Basic French knot
Work in any direction:
Bring needle up at **1**. Holding thread taut with finger and thumb of left hand, wind thread once or twice (not more) quite tightly around needle tip.
Still holding the thread, insert needle very close to point **1** and pull needle through to back of work so the twists lie neatly on the fabric surface. Repeat as required.

OTHER DECORATIVE MACHINE STITCHES

Appliqués can be finished with any of the decorative stitches found on your sewing machine. You'll find that these will vary depending on which machine you have, but most machines have at least a small selection. Practice and play around on some scrap fabrics to find the stitches and widths you like best. Experiment with different threads too—using matching or contrasting thread produces distinctly different looks. Why not write down your favorite settings in your personal sewing journal so they will be handy when you begin your next project. (See page 118 for how to make a sewing journal.)

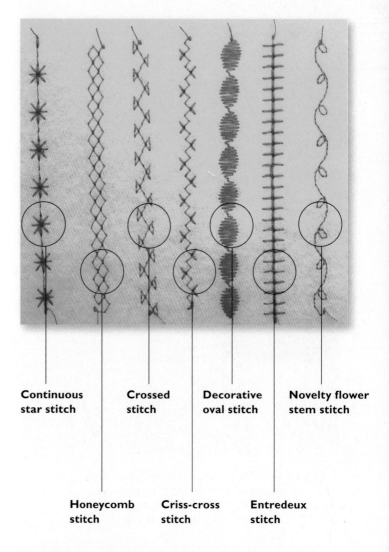

Continuous star stitch

Crossed stitch

Decorative oval stitch

Novelty flower stem stitch

Honeycomb stitch

Criss-cross stitch

Entredeux stitch

EMBELLISHMENTS

Beads, sequins, glue-on gems, wobbly eyes, ribbons, and trims can all be added to an appliqué to personalize it and make it even more outstanding. There are no rules here so let your imagination take over!

MATERIALS

- Button(s) of your choice
- Needle and thread or embellishment glue

BUTTONS

These are available in hundreds if not thousands of designs. They can have two holes, or four holes, or they can have shanks on the back—and they can be just about any color or shape you can think of. You can even get fancy designs, such as the leaf buttons used for Woodland Maple (page 69). You can use buttons just for decoration, as on Buttoned-up Disco Ball (page 55) or to indicate something round, like the center of a flower or the eyes of an animal (see It's All Fantasy, page 88). The fancy buttons, of course, should be used according to their design.

Sometimes one or two embellishments are all you need. At other times you just can't overdo it, as on this Button Berry strawberry motif (page 108), where the mass of buttons creates a luscious look.

Using buttons as embellishments

Buttons can be glued on, but if you know the finished project will have a lot of use or will go through the laundry, it is better to sew them on with a couple of stitches.

Using glue

When using embellishment glue to attach buttons to your project, read the label and make sure that you're using a glue that will dry clear. You don't want white glue visible through the buttonholes!

Using stitches

For strength and durability, use a needle and thread to attach your button to the appliqué or base fabric. Just take a few stitches from the back of the fabric through the buttonholes—you'll know when it feels secure.

Tip

Lay out your embellishment(s) on the appliqué before sewing. Experiment with different combinations before you commit by sewing or gluing them down. Choose your embellishments according to the use and care of your final project.

SEQUINS AND TINY BEADS

Adding sequins is an easy way to add sparkle. Standard sequins are round, come in many plain colors, and can be bought loose in packs, in strips, or even as a fabric. You can also buy them in metallic, iridescent, and even holographic varieties, as well as in various fancy shapes such as hearts, flowers, shells, angels, and more. Each sequin has a hole in the center, where it gets stitched down. There are several ways of attaching sequins, and you can even do it by machine, but below is one of the simplest and most effective methods for our purposes.

MATERIALS

- Sequins of your choice
- Small matching or contrasting beads
- Needle and thread

Attaching sequins

You can attach sequins simply by taking one stitch through the center, but a neater—and more interesting—result can be achieved by using a small bead as a "stop."

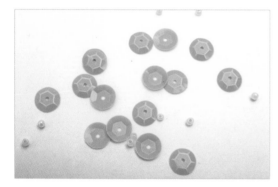

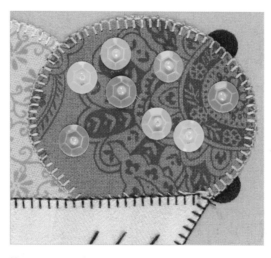

Here, a scattering of sequins suggests the sprinkles on top of an ice cream scoop. They sparkle enticingly in the light, adding a fresh element to the design. Attaching them is easy—just follow the instructions that begin to your left. This motif, Twice as Nice, can be found on page 112.

1 Scatter your sequins on a flat surface to make it easy to see the cupped sides. When sewing the sequins on, the cupped sides should be on top.

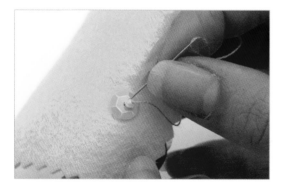

2 Take a needle and thread of a color that doesn't stand out too much. Make sure your needle is small enough to fit through the beads. Knot the thread. Starting on the wrong side of your project, push the needle through the fabric, then through the sequin. Add a small bead and thread back through the hole in the sequin.

3 Repeat this process to attach all the required sequins. Keep some space between them. Knot the thread on the back of the fabric when done. Sewing sequins may take a while, but it gives awesome results.

FABRIC FLOWERS

You can make fabric flowers yourself (see "Three-dimensional fabric folding" on page 36) but as embellishments there are many ready made fabric flowers to be found in craft stores. These are often made of a fine fabric, such as organza or ribbon, and the fancier versions can be multilayered or beaded. You can use fabric glue to attach them or, for a more secure finish, hand sew them on.

Here, a fabric flower is used as a pretty hair ornament for this fine lady who is based on Watching Over Me, page 78. You can glue on a flower like this or, if it doesn't already have a bead in the center, you can stitch it on in the same way as a sequin (see "Attaching sequins," page 49), giving the flower a pretty center which is attached in one easy move.

TRIMMING RIBBON ENDS

The long edges of ribbon won't unravel but the ends might. You can either tuck the ends under and glue them down out of sight, or treat them as explained here.

Trim the ends of the ribbon using sharp scissors for perfect cuts. If your ribbon tends to fray, use a small amount of anti-fray solution on the ends. You can make the cuts in a variety of ways, as shown here.

RIBBON BOWS

Ribbons can be folded into bows as extra embellishment to decorate any item. You can tie a standard bow, but these neat, flat bows are particularly attractive.

To tie a bow like this, cut three strips of different-sized ribbon. In this example, 6 in. (15 cm), 5 in. (13 cm), and 1 in. (2½ cm) strips are used. Loop the longest strip with both ends slightly overlapping, and fold flat. Attach the ends with a dot of fabric glue keeping the glued ends in the middle on the bottom. Do the same for the medium-sized strip. Place this on top of the larger one. The small strip of ribbon is then folded around both ribbon pieces. Glue the ends of the small ribbon piece together on the center bottom.

APPLIQUÉ TIPS

1 FINE TUNING
Before beginning an appliqué, set up your machine with the thread you plan to use. Always sew a sample using the stitch and fabrics you will be using for the appliqué, and then you can adjust your thread tension, stitch width, and length so that it matches the look you have in mind.

2 FINGERTIP TIP
Use your fingertips to gently guide the fabric while sewing with the machine. No matter how fast or slow you sew, too much pressure on the fabric prevents it from moving easily under the needle.

3 FABRIC JOURNAL
Use a journal to write down your favorite stitches and settings. Make it a reference guide of fabrics you've used. Glue or staple a sample of your fabric on a page and write what it is, where you got it from, and what you made of it. Add your experiences—did it shrink a lot? Did it fray? This will give you great insight into your fabrics and their qualities.

4 SEWING AROUND CURVES
At curves, slow down your speed and use your hands to steer the fabric. Sometimes it is necessary to stop stitching and reposition. Drop your needle on the outside of the curve, raise the presser foot and reposition the fabric. This will ensure a fluid curve.

5 SEWING CORNERS
When you approach a corner, stitch to the end and drop your needle into the outside of the edge. Now raise the presser foot and line up your fabric in the direction you need to go. Lower the presser foot and continue stitching.

6 PROPER BONDING
Especially for clothing or other practical projects, be sure the appliqué is secured along the edges, and that the supporting material can hold the appliqué, to endure daily use. A heavily beaded embellishment should not be attached to very delicate base fabric because the weight of the appliqué will distort the fabric.

7 FINDING INSPIRATION
Give yourself time to daydream—great ideas take time. Explore new materials. Don't think about success or failure, just try.

8 PRACTICE, PRACTICE, PRACTICE
Everything gets better with practice and experience. The more you appliqué, the better you will get.

9 MORE THAN YOU NEED
If possible, start with a larger base fabric than your finished design, as appliqué can distort the background size. You can always trim off any excess afterward.

10 COORDINATE
For the best effect, choose the colors and patterns of the appliqué to suit the overall design. A tiny, detailed appliqué will be lost in a busy project, while a plainer base fabric will highlight it.

CHAPTER THREE

In these pages, you'll find over 100 appliqué designs, grouped into five themed sections for easy reference. Pick a motif you like, dive into your stash, and get appliquéing! Refer back to the Motif Selector on pages 8–11 to choose your favorite design.

DESIGN & PATTERN DIRECTORY

MOTIFS 1–14   ALL SHAPES AND SIZES

Squares, circles, triangles, oblongs, stars—these simple shapes create wonderful patterns for appliqué motifs. The following section will introduce you to basic color appliqué designs, which you can apply to anything from bookbags to wall art to accessories, and everything else you can imagine.

1 BUTTONED-UP DISCO BALL

Dive into your bag of buttons and look for seven different bright buttons of a similar size to embellish this whorl of spots and circles.

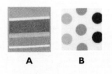

A
B

A   Cut one large circle
B   Cut one small circle

METHOD

Machine   Fused

page 26

Work satin stitch around the large circle and zigzag stitch on the edge of the smaller circle.

Additional materials

Hand sew seven buttons in place around the small central circle.

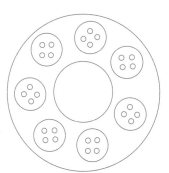

2 CATHEDRAL WINDOW

This basic motif recalls the design of a cathedral window patchwork and features a circle with a diamond in the center. It's much easier than it looks.

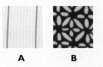

A
B

A   Cut one square background block
B   Cut four symmetrical curved shapes

METHOD

Machine   Fused

page 26

Lay the four curved shapes on top of material A, and arrange in a circle, before machine stitching into place.

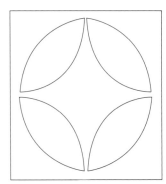

3 YOU'RE A STAR!

This popular motif works well on any project and it's suitable for everyone, so get stitching.

A

A   Cut one square of fabric large enough to easily cover the entire star shape

METHOD

Machine   Reverse

▶ page 32

Choose a decorative stitch to work around the star—a series of small stars work well, or you could work cross stitches, or simply use running stitch.

> ### Tips
> For more on decorative machine stitches, see pages 40–47.

4 THE HEART OF THE MATTER

Circles and curves combine here to create a soft design with a heart at its middle. Simple stitching in complementary colors is an elegant finishing touch.

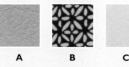

A   **B**   **C**

A   Cut one heart
B   Cut one circle
C   Cut one flower shape

METHOD

Machine   Fused

▶ page 26

Lay out the fabric cuts in the order indicated on the template, right. Fuse all parts and finish edges of the heart and flower border with a blanket stitch. Use a satin stitch on the edge of the circle for variation.

5 HEXAGON FLOWER

6 CHRYSALIS

The shapes used in this motif are associated with traditional patchwork and have a quaint, homespun feel. Here they have been arranged to create a six-petaled flower.

Hearts and ovals combine to create a geometric pattern that resembles a butterfly emerging from its chrysalis. Contrasting topstitching enhances the shapes.

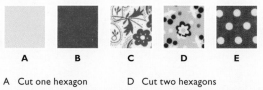

A	B	C	D	E

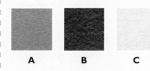

A	B	C

A Cut one hexagon
B Cut one hexagon
C Cut one hexagon
D Cut two hexagons
E Cut two hexagons

A Cut one oval and two small hearts
B Cut two ovals and two medium hearts
C Cut two large hearts

METHOD

Machine Fused

▶ page 26

Finish with satin stitches on the edge of each hexagon.

METHOD

Hand Fused

▶ page 26

Use running stitches and backstitches on the different shapes for decorative effect.

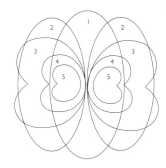

> **Tip**
> When you are cutting material, make sure you keep all scraps: they can make wonderful small features in any future appliqué project.

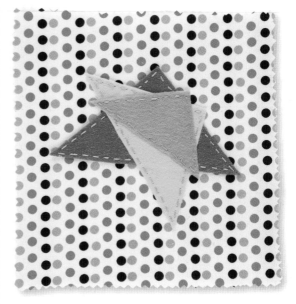

7 FRAYED OBLONGS

8 TRIPLE TRIANGLES

The frayed edges of these simple oblong shapes have a soft, homely look. Choose fabrics which fray easily, such as cotton, linen, or rayon, and use the raw edge technique.

Take a simple geometric shape—a triangle—cut it into different sizes, and appliqué. It couldn't be easier and it's great fun. Use clashing or contrasting fabrics to your taste.

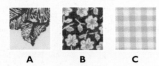

A   Cut one large oblong
B   Cut one medium oblong
C   Cut one small oblong

A   Cut one small triangle
B   Cut one medium triangle
C   Cut one large triangle

METHOD

page 30

Fraying works best after every element is sewn in place. First decide how long you want the fringe to be: make your first stitch so far away from the edge. Use a pin to tease out the threads beyond the stitching line. Frays will look better after a wash.

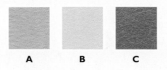

METHOD

page 30

Pin the triangles in place and hand stitch, working small running stitches a short distance from the edge.

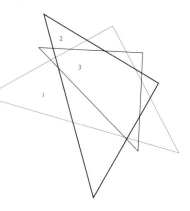

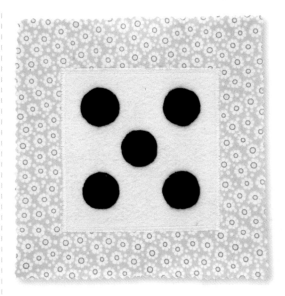

9 HIPPY CHIC

Layer felt circles to create a stunning '70s-look appliqué. Opt for typical retro colors like orange and shades of brown, cream, and green.

A   **B**   **C**   **D**

A Cut four large circles and one small circle
B Cut four medium-large circles
C Cut four medium circles

METHOD

Machine   Raw edge

page 30

Pin one small circle onto one medium circle. Sew a straight stitch inside the edge. Pin this onto the medium-large circle, and sew secure. Pin on the large circle and sew secure. Repeat four times. Arrange all circles on the base fabric. Sew the remaining small circle to the middle.

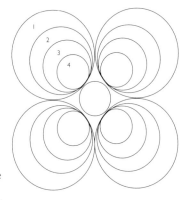

10 LUCKY DICE

What's your lucky number? Appliqué a square for the base of the die, and glue on your preferred number of dots. For best results, choose contrasting colors.

A   **B**

A Cut one square
B Cut your chosen number of dots

METHOD

Machine   Raw edge

page 30

Pin material A in place on the base fabric, and finish the edges with matching satin stitch. Glue the dots in place, spacing them evenly.

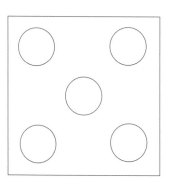

> **Tip**
> If you are gluing on any details, like the dots here, the glue should help prevent fraying. To be sure, choose a non-fraying fabric or apply a little anti-fray solution.

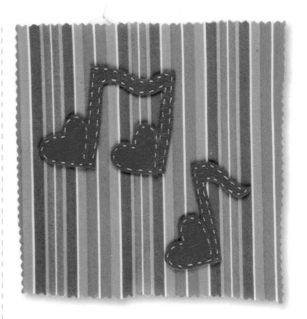

11 LOST IN SPACE

Like the planets of a solar system, four small circles revolve around a larger, brighter one, which has been highlighted with decorative edge stitching.

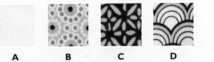

| A | B | C | D |

A Cut one piece of fabric large enough to easily cover the largest circle

B Cut two small circles
C Cut one small circle
D Cut one small circle

METHOD

Machine   Reverse   Fused

▸ page 32   ▸ page 26

Use the reverse appliqué technique on the large circle and fuse the other circles in place. Be careful when ironing on vinyl fabrics. Finish all circles with a decorative stitch of your choice.

Tip
For more on decorative machine stitches, see pages 40–47.

12 LOVE NOTES

These musical hearts are easy-to-make and would be a perfect gift for someone just starting to learn an instrument.

A

A Cut the music note bases and three hearts

METHOD

Hand   Fused   Raw edge

▸ page 26   ▸ page 30

Fuse the pieces in place, with the bases under the hearts, and use running stitch to decorate the edges by hand.

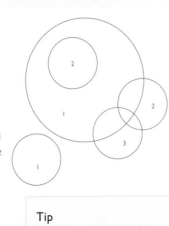

13 THE HEART WITHIN

Pinking shears will help prevent fabric edges from fraying, but cut edges often look good too. So pink away and show off those edgy edges with this heart within a heart.

14 SEGMENTED HEXAGON

In this design, six triangles meet at the center of a larger hexagon. Placed at different angles on a project, or tessellated, this appliqué would add a sense of movement.

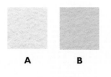

A   **B**

A   Cut one large heart
B   Cut one small heart

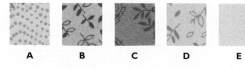

A   **B**   **C**   **D**   **E**

A   Cut one hexagon   D   Cut one triangle
B   Cut two triangles   E   Cut one triangle
C   Cut two triangles

METHOD

Machine   Raw edge

▸ page 30

Use pinking shears to cut the hearts to the desired size. Sew in place with a straight stitch a little way from the edges of each template.

Additional materials
Stitch a ribbon rose to the central heart, close to the top edge as a finishing touch.

Tip
Use a decorative button or another trimming of your choice, instead of a ribbon rose.

METHOD

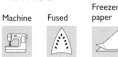

Machine   Fused   Freezer paper

▸ page 26   ▸ page 28

Use the freezer paper method for the hexagon and then fuse the triangles on top. Add decorative stitching, if desired.

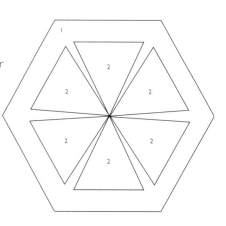

THE NATURAL COLLECTION

Journey through the great outdoors in this collection of appliqué motifs that feature floral patterns and natural shapes suitable for adorning camping and outdoor gear. Think green!—recycle your leftover scraps of fabric and you'll create some great results.

The natural collection **63**

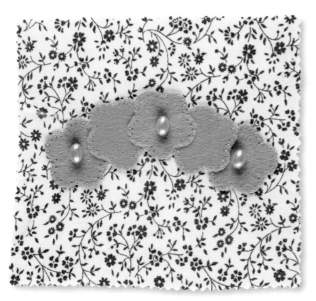

15 PEARLY FLOWER BORDER

The simple flower shapes used in this decorative motif will be used over and over in this section. Sew five flowers together in an overlapping line to create a pretty border, adding pearl beads to their centers to catch the eye.

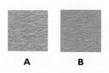

A Cut three flowers
B Cut two flowers

METHOD

Hand Raw edge

page 30

Use blanket stitch around every flower in a contrasting color.

Additional materials
Sew a bead to every flower cut from fabric A.

16 EVERLASTING CACTUS

Cacti, like people, come in many shapes and sizes—and some of them are pricklier than others. Add as many hand embroidered spikes as you wish to personalize your cactus motif.

A Cut one cactus
B Cut one pot

METHOD

Hand Fused

page 26

Work blanket stitch all around the edge of the flowerpot and the cactus. Hand embroider the spikes as you please.

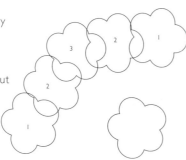

> **Tip**
> This motif could also be used to create an egg in an eggcup for Easter. Just choose appropriate fabrics and omit the embroidered prickles.

17 WHITE HIBISCUS

This cute hibiscus flower would look lovely on a bag, hat, cushion, and many other items. It's cut in one piece but the folded leaves and button center give added dimension.

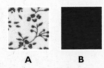

A   B

A   Cut one flower
A   Cut two leaves

METHOD

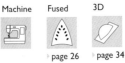

Machine   Fused   3D

▸ page 26   ▸ page 34

Fuse the flower in place and stitch a narrow zigzag around the edges. Fold the leaves and sew them down the center with a straight stitch.

Additional materials
Glue a large button to the center of the flower.

18 FIVE-LEAVED DAISY

This single, long-stemmed flower combines colorful felts and easy straight stitches. (See the Super Sunflower variation, right.)

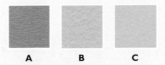

A   B   C

A   Cut five leaves
B   Cut one flower shape
C   Cut one round flower center

METHOD

Machine   Raw edge

▸ page 30

Arrange the pieces on the base fabric and mark where the stem should fall. Work zigzag stitch as the stem. Pin all parts in place and sew down with straight stitch.

> ### Tip
> Add dimension by using folded leaves as on motif 17, left.

19 TULIPS IN BLOOM

These cheerful tulips have wobbly rickrack stems and sun-striped leaves, and will brighten up any project.

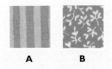

A   **B**

A   Cut four leaves
A   Cut three tulip flowers

METHOD

Hand   **Fused**   **Raw edge**

▶ page 26   ▶ page 30

Position all the elements of the flowers before applying them. Work blanket stitches around the leaves and backstitches on the flowers in coordinating colors.

Additional materials
Glue the rickrack trim in place between the flowers and leaves.

Variation

18
SUPER SUNFLOWER

Reaching up to the sun, this super long version of motif 18 has nine leaves and a long, strong ribbon stem. You could make it even longer, if desired, and even add more flowers along the way.

Mix and Match

16 + 17
DAPPER DAYLILY

Use the pot template of motif 16 to grow any other plant or flower. Here it's been replaced with a red version of the White Hibiscus flower (motif 17).

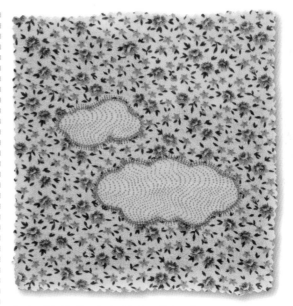

20 PINK MUSHROOMS

This pink mushroom design is worked using pink and white vinyl fabrics trimmed with pretty ribbon roses.

21 DREAMY CLOUDS

Always walking with your head in the clouds? Have a go at this dreamy, easy-to-make reverse appliqué.

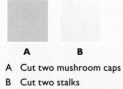

A   **B**

A   Cut two mushroom caps
B   Cut two stalks

A

A   Cut a piece large enough to easily cover both clouds

METHOD

Machine

Pin the parts in place and sew satin stitches in coordinating colors all round the edges.

Additional materials
Hand sew a ribbon rose to the right-hand corner of each mushroom cap.

Tips
Instead of using ribbon roses, sew on small red or white buttons to resemble the spots on a toadstool.

METHOD

Machine   **Reverse**

▸ page 32

Finish the edges with blanket stitch worked with the long stitches facing outward.

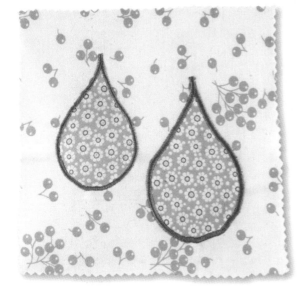

22 FALLING RAINDROPS

23 SNACKS FOR SQUIRRELS

It's raining but don't worry, you'll find an umbrella on page 80. These simple shapes can be applied using the padded appliqué technique and are easily enlarged or reduced.

The acorn is a great shape to apply using the freezer paper technique. This motif would look especially good on items for the kitchen, camping, or outdoor eating.

A

A Cut two drop shapes

A   **B**

A Cut one acorn cup
B Cut one acorn and one stem

METHOD

Machine   3D

▸ page 36

Finish with satin stitch around all edges.

METHOD

Machine   Fused   Freezer paper

▸ page 26   ▸ page 28

Both main parts of the acorn are applied using the freezer paper technique. Finish by fusing the small stem on top.

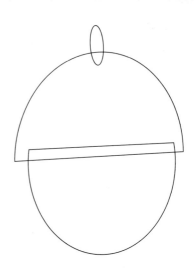

24 BUTTON TREE

Use cute buttons to embellish this graphic tree. Go for decorative buttons in flower or fruit shapes, but if these are not available, brightly colored buttons will work well, too.

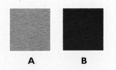

A   B

A   Cut one tree canopy
B   Cut one tree trunk

METHOD

Machine   Fused

▸ page 26

Work satin stitch, making sure it is not too narrow, around both the trunk and the tree canopy.

Additional materials
Glue on the decorative buttons, adding fallen fruits, if desired.

25 SCRAP FOREST TREE

This design will use up your small fabric scraps. Play around with different green fabrics until you find the most pleasing combination.

A   B   C   D

A   Cut one tree trunk
B   Cut two top pieces (left and right)
C   Cut one top piece (upper middle)
D   Cut one top piece (lower middle)

METHOD

Machine   Fused

▸ page 26

Use narrow blanket stitch on all visible edges of both the trunk and the sections of the tree canopy.

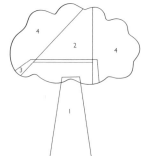

Tips
Want to save some time? Appliqué the treetop out of one shape as in motif 24, left. This method is also used in Owl's Hideout—the mix and match design on page 91.

26 WOODLAND MAPLE

27 WATER LILIES IN WINTER

Made from just one hand stitched shape, this appliqué design is extremely easy to make. The rich colors and maple leaf buttons evoke a forest in the Fall.

There's something particularly appealing and satisfying about a single leaf shape. This generously proportioned leaf is embellished with flowers to resemble a leaf in a lily pond. (See the summer variation on page 71.)

A

A   Cut one tree shape

A

A   Cut one piece of fabric large enough
to easily cover the entire leaf shape

METHOD

Hand   Raw edge

▸ page 30

Stitch blanket stitch around the edge of the tree in a toning color.

Additional materials
Sew on two wooden leaf shaped buttons—these maple leaves enhance the seasonal color scheme.

METHOD

Machine   Reverse

▸ page 32

Sew satin stitch on leaf in a curved line as a center vein. Work zigzag stitch around the leaf.

Additional materials
Glue on small fabric flowers.

28 SPRING CROCUS

The loose petals create a three-dimensional effect on this super spring flower. Since the back of the petals can be seen, use different fabrics on the front and back. Apply this motif to a hat or shoe on page 122.

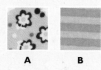

A   **B**

A   Cut five petals for the front of the flower
B   Cut five petals for the back of the flower (not shown here)

METHOD

Machine   3D

▸ page 34

Additional materials

Cut five petal flowers in each material. Fuse the front petal to the back petal using fusible web. Gather the base of the petals in a central point and fasten with a single stitch. Finish with a button at the center of the flower.

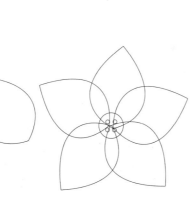

29 FLOWERS OF FALL

Big, bold fabric prints lend themselves to easy appliqué. Find motifs with a shared theme, like these autumnal flowers.

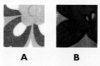

A   **B**

A   Cut around your chosen fabric print
B   Cut around your chosen fabric print

METHOD

Machine   Raw edge

▸ page 30

Cut the desired flower prints from your fabrics and then use the raw-edge appliqué technique to attach them to the base fabric. Finish the edges with satin and straight stitches, or the stitch of your choice.

You'll find ready made templates in basic fabric prints. Select the shape you like, and cut carefully around the outline.

30 EVERGREEN FLOWER

One petal shape cut six times in two different colors makes a simple but effective design. Choose fabrics linked by color or design, and finish with some simple beading.

A   **B**

A   Cut four flower petals
B   Cut two flower petals

METHOD

Hand   Raw edge

page 30

Attach the petals by hand with backstitch.

Additional materials
Sew small beads around the edges of alternating petals, in short stitches.

Variation

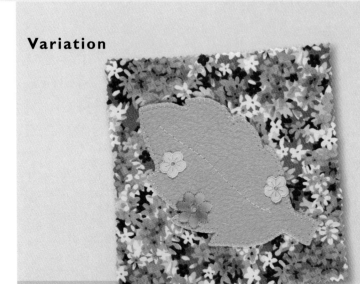

27

WATER LILIES IN SUMMER

Here, the leaf shape from motif 27 has been attached using the raw edge appliqué method, and hand stitched in place. Fabric flowers add the finishing touch.

Use it here

19 + 11

DOTTY TEA TOWEL

Spice up plain dish towels with an appliqué design like this arrangement of rickrack trim, circles, and leaves.

31 GEOMETRIC FLOWER

Radiating from a central circle, this geometric flower has six stems, each tipped with a button blossom. Choose bright and sunny colored buttons for a lively look to any project.

A

A   Cut one circle

METHOD

Machine   Fused

▶ page 26

Fuse the inner circle in place and edge with blanket stitch. Sew six stems forking out from the circle with a decorative machine stitch.

Additional materials
Select six buttons of similar size and sew to the end of each stem.

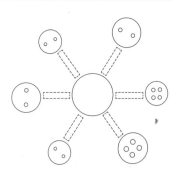

Tip
As an alternative to decorative machine stitching, use strips of ribbon for the stems.

32 FLORAL ROSETTE

This rosette's a real winner, and its petaled edges give it a unique, handmade appearance. Look out for ribbon suitable for your theme or occasion.

A   **B**

A   Cut one circle
B   Cut one petaled rosette shape

METHOD

Hand   Raw edge

▶ page 30

Additional materials
Cut two strips of ribbon. Pin the rosette pieces in place with the strips of ribbon at least ½ in. (1.2 mm) under the rosette. Finish the petaled rosette with backstitch, securing the ribbons at the same time, and finish the center circle with blanket stitch.

33 DAZZLING RIBBON FLOWERS

Make super fast three-dimensional flowers by cutting and folding strips of ribbon. Hide the joining stitches in the center with a pretty button.

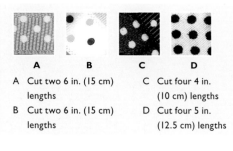

A	B	C	D

A Cut two 6 in. (15 cm) lengths

B Cut two 6 in. (15 cm) lengths

C Cut four 4 in. (10 cm) lengths

D Cut four 5 in. (12.5 cm) lengths

METHOD

Hand   3D

page 34

Lay four ribbons of the same length right side down in a star-like arrangement. Insert a threaded needle down through the center, catching all the ribbons through the middle. Fold the ends of one strip in toward the center to form two loops; sew the ends in place. Repeat to form the remaining petals. Make several additional stitches through the center of the ribbon flower to secure the layers.

Additional materials

Finish each flower with a button at the center.

Mix and Match

30 + 33

3D FLOWER

This three-dimensional flower is a lively combination of motif 30 on page 71 (now in two complementary pink color tones), and motif 33, left.

4 + 3

BRIGHT STAR

Insert a star in the center of motif 4 instead of a heart to create a variation of the Floral Rosette, left. Notice how the star really stands out because the other two shapes are so close in color that they almost blend into each other.

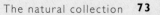

BOYS AND GIRLS COME OUT TO PLAY

It's playtime in this chapter, which features a parade of chic girls, and fashionable boys. Kit out these dolly templates in clothes and accessories of your choice, and learn how to add personality and character to your design with detailed hand embroidery.

34 WAVING BOY

This boy doll is ready to meet some new friends. The appliqué parts in this motif are quite small, but he's relatively easy to make.

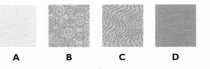

A   Cut all the body parts: face, neck, arms, and feet
B   Cut the hair
C   Cut the dungarees
D   Cut one pocket

METHOD

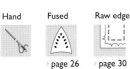

Hand   Fused   Raw edge

▶ page 26   ▶ page 30

Fuse all the pieces in place, starting with the neck and other body parts, and then adding the hair, dungarees, and finally the pocket. Finish the boy's outfit with running stitch. Use backstitch on the pocket and boy's hair. Embroider the facial features.

35 WAVING GIRL

Use the same template from motif 34 to create this fashionable girl doll. Dress her up in your favorite colors, or change her coloring to resemble someone you know.

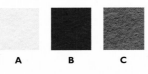

A   Cut all body parts: face, neck, arms, and legs
B   Cut the hair
C   Cut one dress and two sleeves

METHOD

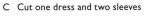

Fused

▶ page 26

Fuse all the pieces in place, starting with the neck and other body parts and then adding the hair, dress, and sleeves. Embroider the facial features.

Additional materials
Stitch two tiny buttons to the front of the dress and add a ribbon trim along the lower edge.

36 PRETTY RED DRESS

37 BASEBALL BUDDY

The hair and dress of this delightful doll are decorated with store-bought flower embellishments.

Ready to work out in his sweatsuit and sports cap, this boy motif is perfect for anyone who loves to be active and play sports. Change the colors to suit the team you support.

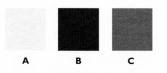

A   B   C

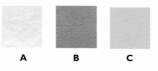

A   B   C

A   Cut all the body parts: face, neck, arms, and legs
B   Cut the hair
C   Cut one dress and two sleeves

A   Cut all the body parts: face, neck, arms, and feet
B   Cut the pants and cap
C   Cut one shirt and one cap band

METHOD

Hand   Fused   Raw edge

▸ page 26   ▸ page 30

Fuse all pieces in place, starting with the neck and other body parts. Add the hair, dress, and sleeves. Decorate the dress with backstitches along the edges, and embroider the eyes and mouth.

Additional materials
Use a single stitch to secure fabric flower embellishments.

METHOD

Hand   Raw edge

▸ page 30

Glue all parts of the appliqué onto the base fabric. Finish the boy's outfit with hand stitches: running stitch on the shirt; backstitches on the pants and cap; and an embroidered backstitch circle on the shirt. Embroider the eyes, mouth and hair.

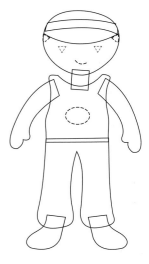

38 DANCING WITH BUTTERFLIES

This bright and cheerful doll is adorned with butterfly charms to create a jolly composition perfect for spring or summer.

A   B   C

A   Cut all body parts: face, neck, arms, and legs

B   Cut the hair

C   Cut one dress

METHOD

Machine   Fused   Raw edge

▸page 26   ▸page 30

Fuse all the pieces in place, starting with the neck and other body parts. Then add the hair and dress. Finish the hair and dress shapes with satin stitches in matching threads. Embroider the facial features.

Additional materials
Glue on an assortment of fabric butterfly charms.

Mix and Match

37 + 38

HANGING OUT THE WASHING

Laundry day! Here, the dolls' clothes are hung out to dry. The washing line is attached with a zigzag stitch. Use the shirt and trousers from motif 37 and the dress from motif 38, or add your own clothes designs to the line.

77 + 36 + 38

CART RIDE

Use the cart from motif 77 on page 100 and pop your doll of choice inside—this girl was made using elements from various different dolls: motif 36, dress and hair; motif 38, arms.

39 WATCHING OVER ME

40 TIME FOR WORK

Add character to your motifs with a pair of wobbly eyes. This little lady wears her hair tied in a neat bun, adorned here with a pretty ribbon-rose trim.

This smart young man is ready to go to the office. He's the same basic shape as motif 39, but the details are different.

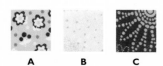

A   **B**   **C**

A   Cut one triangular body
B   Cut one face
C   Cut the hair and hair bun

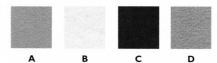

A   **B**   **C**   **D**

A   Cut one triangular body
B   Cut one face
C   Cut the hair

D   Cut two round eyes and the
    two parts of the necktie

METHOD

Machine   Freezer paper

▸ page 28

Apply the pieces using the freezer paper technique and then embroider the mouth.

Additional materials
Add stick-on wobbly eyes and a ribbon-rose trim.

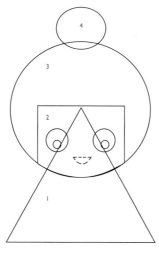

METHOD

Hand   Fused   Raw edge

▸ page 26   ▸ page 30

Finish with running stitch around the major shapes (body, head, and hair). Embroider facial details.

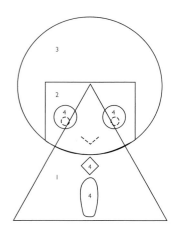

41 POSH AND PRETTY

Shiny craft embellishments add personality to this motif. If you don't have gems for the eyes, try sequins or beads.

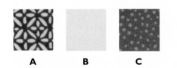

A   B   C

A   Cut one triangular body
B   Cut one face
C   Cut the hair and two buns

METHOD

Machine   Fused

▶ page 26

Finish with satin stitches in matching threads. Embroider the mouth.

Additional materials
Use embellishment glue to attach two sparkly gems for the eyes and another gem for the dress button.

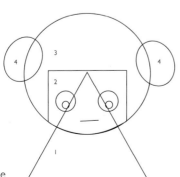

42 PRECIOUS ANGEL

This pink angel appliqué is dressed in pink but she'd look just as good in blue, gold, or any of your favorite colors.

A   B   C   D

A   Cut one body   D   Cut one head
B   Cut two wings
C   Cut one face

METHOD

Hand   Machine   Freezer paper

▶ page 28

Use the freezer paper technique to attach the body, wings, and head. Next, embroider the facial features and pin the face in place, securing it with running stitch.

Additional materials
Create a headband with a row of five sequins, attaching each one with a small bead in the center.

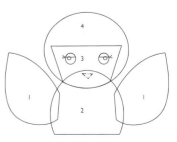

43 STRAWBERRY CLUTCH

44 RAIN OR SHINE

Where is an appliquéd doll to leave all her daily necessaries? This pretty clutch is applied using reverse appliqué and has a cord handle fixed with zigzag stitch.

This umbrella, or parasol, is quick and easy to make. Add embellishments if desired, or mix and match with the Falling Raindrops (motif 22) design on page 67.

A   **B**

A   Cut a piece of fabric large enough to easily cover entire bag shape
B   Cut one bag closure tab

A   **B**

A   Cut one umbrella handle
B   Cut one umbrella top

METHOD

Machine   Fused   Reverse

▶ page 26   ▶ page 32

Fuse the closure tab onto fabric A. Work reverse appliqué on the purse shape. Finish all edges with satin stitch.

Additional materials
Glue button onto tab. Arrange the cord trimming in a handle shape and attach with fabric glue. Sew zigzag stitch over the handle.

METHOD

Machine   Fused   3D

▶ page 26   ▶ page 34

Fuse handle in place and sew a short blanket stitch all around. Add dimension by using the padded technique on the top part.

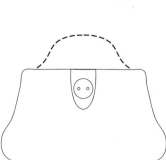

45 SLEEPING BEAUTY

Simple appliquéd circles and egg shapes make up this picture of calm and contentment. Embroider the eyes and eyelashes by hand for a delicate finishing touch.

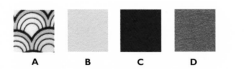

A   Cut one egg shape   D   Cut two round cheeks
B   Cut two hands and one face
C   Cut the hair

METHOD

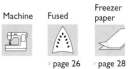

▸ page 26   ▸ page 28

Start by using the freezer paper technique on the egg shape. Embroider the eyes and eyelashes on the face and then fuse the face and remaining pieces onto the egg.

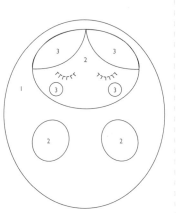

46 HAPPY VALENTINE

This motif is ideal for Valentine's Day, but you could use it on any gift. Here, the large oval is cut from pink fake fur fabric.

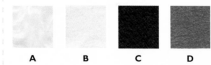

A   Cut one egg shape   D   Cut one heart
B   Cut two hands and one face
C   Cut the hair

METHOD

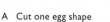

▸ page 26

Use zigzag stitch on the edge of the fake fur fabric. Embroider the eyes and mouth.

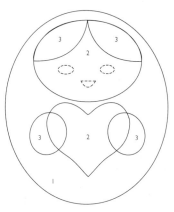

47 EGG GIRL

This egg-shaped girl doll holds a colorful flower, stitched into place with a button at its center. This design will bring an innocent charm to any project.

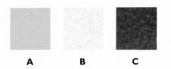

A   **B**   **C**

A   Cut one egg shape
B   Cut two hands and one face
C   Cut the hair

METHOD

Hand   Raw edge

▶ page 30

Finish main pieces with running stitch and the hair with backstitch.

Additional materials
Arrange a small button on top of a fabric flower and stitch in place between the hands.

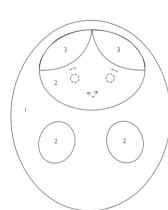

48 CREAMY KOKESHI

Kokeshi are typical Japanese dolls. Although traditionally Kokeshi didn't have arms or legs, contemporary Kokeshi dolls allow you complete freedom of design. Why not mix this design with motifs 49 and 50 to create a family of Kokeshi?

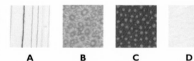

A   **B**   **C**   **D**

A   Cut one body, two sleeves, and the hair
B   Cut one belt piece
C   Cut one belt piece
D   Cut one face

METHOD

Machine   3D

▶ page 34

Finish with satin stitches. Embroider the facial features.

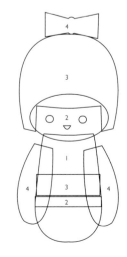

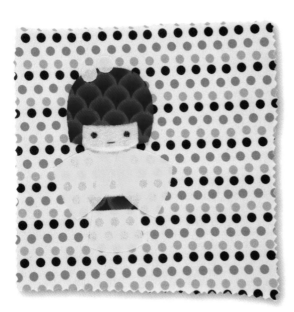

49 YELLOW YUKATA

This Kokeshi doll is ready for bed in her yellow yukata robe. Yellow is the color of courage in Japan, so she'll embolden your project and bring only sweet dreams.

A	B	C

A   Cut one body, two sleeves, and two small circles
B   Cut one face
C   Cut one belt and the hair

METHOD

Fused

▸ page 26

Work French knots for the eyes and embroider the mouth in running stitch.

Tip
Give your Kokeshi a parasol, right.

Mix and Match

44 + 49

KIMONO AND UMBRELLA

Whatever the weather, you'll find the umbrella on page 80 and the doll in motif 49, left.

Use it here

17 + 47

PADDED WALL HANGING

Combine motifs of your choice to make a delightful soft wall hanging. Add two ribbon loops on top of the padded project so you can hang it on the wall. This example uses a variation of the White Hibiscus flower from page 64 and the Egg Girl from page 82. See pages 124–125 for more details on how to make your wall hanging.

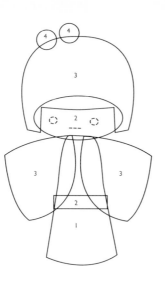

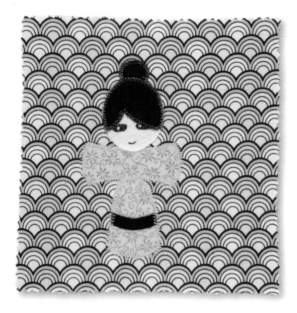

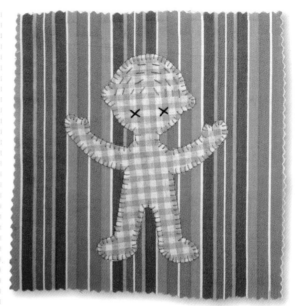

50 KIMONO GIRL

Kokeshi dolls are also lucky charms, so appliqué this stylish motif on any project to bring good luck.

51 BASIC BOY

This one-part-boy is a quick and easy-to-make appliqué. Details can be left out to give the impression of a silhouette, or more detail can be added; try adding a button on his belly, or a small piece of trim to indicate a belt.

A   B   C

A   Cut one body shape and one sleeve piece
B   Cut one face
C   Cut one belt, the hair and one bun

A

A   Cut one boy shape

METHOD

Machine   Fused

▸ page 26

Work zigzag stitch around material A. Embroider facial features.

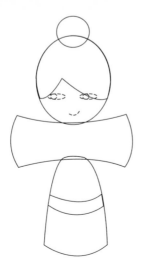

METHOD

Machine   Fused

▸ page 26

Finish the edges of the boy with a machine-worked blanket stitch. Embroider eyes and hair.

52 BASIC GIRL

Work this motif in any color of your choice. If you're short of time, cut the girl from one shape for fast results. Decorate her dress with glued-on buttons for a snappy finish.

A	B

A   Cut one upper body shape
B   Cut two legs

METHOD

Machine   Fused

▸ page 26

Finish the legs with a matching color satin stitch, and the upper body with a blanket stitch. Embroider backstitches for the hair and eyes.

Mix and Match

51 + 52

HIM AND HER

Use whipped running stitches around the edges of motifs 51 and 52. Here, a smaller version of Madame Butterfly (motif 60) on page 90 hovers above the couple. Store-bought fabric butterfly charms are glued on to complete this jolly scene.

39 + 103

LOVE AT FIRST SIGHT

Let the wide-eyed doll from page 78 express her love: combine this motif with the In Your Dreams design (motif 103) on page 115.

CUTE, CUDDLY, AND CURIOUS CREATURES

In this chapter you'll find a wide selection of animals, which will make perfect gifts for young children. Have a go at one-piece appliqués like Kitty Cat or Madame Butterfly first, and then try the multiple-pieced motifs, such as Cheeky Squirrel or Wide-eyed Owl. Experiment with different fabric textures and make them cuddlier than ever!

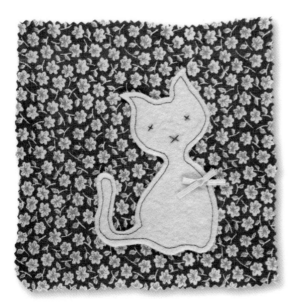

53 KITTY CAT

Anyone can make this simple felt appliqué. It has basic embroidered features and a ready made fabric bow trim.

A

A Cut one cat shape

METHOD

Hand   Raw edge

▸ page 30

Choose your favorite way to attach the appliqué piece: fuse, glue, or pin in place. Then, hand sew backstitch all around material A. Finish by embroidering crosses for the eyes and nose.

Additional materials
Glue on one fabric bow.

54 CHIHUAHUA

This big-eared Chihuahua puppy has button eyes, but you could use wobbly eyes instead if you wish.

A

A Cut one pattern piece

METHOD

Hand   Raw edge

▸ page 30

Hand stitch the Chihuahua in place with backstitch all round. Use running stitch for the nose and to indicate the division between the face and ears.

Additional materials
Glue on two thick buttons as eyes. Fix buttons securely by hand.

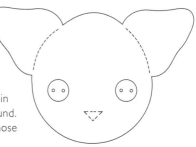

55 IT'S ALL FANTASY

Any shape used in the "All shapes and sizes" chapter can be turned into an appliqué creature. This friendly alien has his arms open wide in a gesture of friendship.

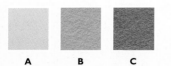

A   B   C

A Cut one body
B Cut two ears
C Cut two arms and two round paws

METHOD

Machine   Fused

▸ page 26

Glue the vinyl body in place and fuse all other parts carefully. Take care not to touch the vinyl with your hot iron. Add narrow blanket stitches around the body and machine sew straight stitches around all other parts.

Additional materials
Glue on two buttons as eyes.

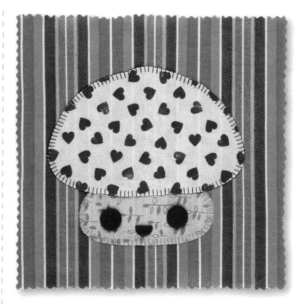

56 HAPPY MUSHROOM

Embellish your kitchen, picnic, or camping items with this adorable creature, or replicate the design to create a whole mushroom family!

A   B   C

A Cut one cap
B Cut one stalk
C Cut two round eyes and one small mouth shape

METHOD

Machine   Fused

▸ page 26

Fuse all pieces and use your machine to blanket stitch around the main parts of the mushroom.

Tips
If you don't have fabric with little red hearts or polka dots, use red or pink fabric for the cap of the mushroom, cut dots from white fabric, and fuse these on top.

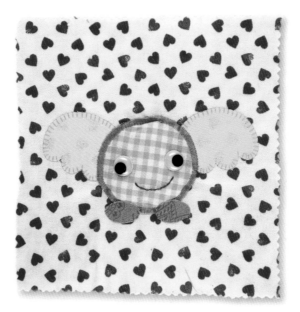

57 SMILEY FACE

This friendly face contains strong shapes and would finish a great project for children, who'll love this little creature.

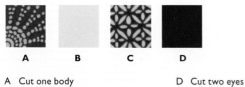

A   **B**   **C**   **D**

A Cut one body   D Cut two eyes
B Cut one face
C Cut two ears

METHOD

Machine   Fused

▸ page 26

Finish all edges except the eyes with satin stitch. Embroider the mouth in backstitch.

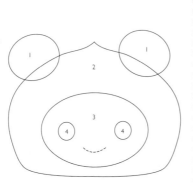

58 WHEN PIGS CAN FLY

This funny little animal flies right out of the fabric. It has a padded head for added dimension and characterful wobbly eyes.

A   **B**   **C**

A Cut one head/body shape
B Cut two wings
C Cut two feet

METHOD

Machine   Fused   3D

▸ page 26   ▸ page 34

Start by fusing the wings in place, then attach the padded circle in the middle. End with the fused feet and embroidered mouth.

Additional materials
Glue on two wobbly eyes.

59 BUMBLING ALONG

This cheerful bee appliqué will brighten up any project. Use freezer paper to get the perfect template, or try this motif in felt, using the raw edge appliqué method.

A   **B**

A Cut one body
B Cut one head and two wings

METHOD

Machine   Freezer paper

▶ page 28

Use the freezer paper appliqué technique for the body, the head, and the wings. Embroider the antennae and stinger.

Additional materials
Sew on two buttons for eyes.

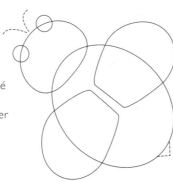

60 MADAME BUTTERFLY

This butterfly template is a great shape to embellish, and offers you much scope for creativity. Beads, buttons, sparkly stones, embroidery—anything goes!

A

A Cut one butterfly shape

METHOD

Machine   Raw edge

▶ page 30

Straight stitch all around material A. Decorate with embroidered circles.

Additional materials
Glue on cord as the antennae and stick on sparkly gems, or other suitable embellishments.

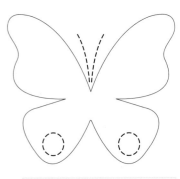

Tip
Printed fabric doesn't need any additional embellishments—see the Printed Butterfly, right.

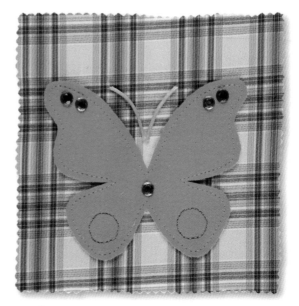

61 | LOVELY LADYBUG

*Ladybugs are said to be lucky and are also symbols of love—
catch and release one, and it should fly straight to your true love.
Why not appliqué this motif as a gift for someone special?*

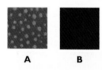

A   B

A   Cut one oval large enough to cover
   the entire ladybug shape
B   Cut one head

METHOD

Machine   Fused   Reverse

▸ page 26   ▸ page 32

Fuse the head onto the body,
which should be cut large enough
to cover the base fabric. Satin
stitch the edge of the head to the
body. Use the reverse appliqué
technique working zigzag stitch all
around. Embroider a line to
divide the wing cases and work
four crossed "dots" on the
ladybug's back.

Variation

60

PRINTED BUTTERFLY

There's no need to add embellishments
if you have a pretty printed fabric,
like the one used here. Select an
appropriate part of the fabric design to
enhance the butterfly. Finish the edges
with satin stitch.

Mix and Match

67 + 25

OWL'S HIDEOUT

Animal motifs and tree designs work
well together. Here, the Wide-eyed
Owl (motif 67) on page 94, is matched
with the Scrap Forest Tree (motif 25)
on page 68. The top of the scrap tree is
cut from one piece of fabric, and so is
the owl's body and perch.

Tip

Small prints usually work
better than large ones.
Think of the actual piece
size when choosing your
printed fabric. Big prints
may lose their appeal
when cut in small shapes.

62 SOFT-SHELLED SNAIL

63 CURIOUS CATERPILLAR

Green fleece makes this snail very soft to the touch, so it's ideal for very young children with exploring fingers. A decorative stitch sewn in circles finishes the snail's shell.

Turn five simple circles into an inquisitive caterpillar. The wobbly eyes add character, as do the hand stitched antennae, which are pricked up and alert.

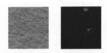

A   **B**

A   Cut one round shell
B   Cut one head and one tail

A   **B**

A   Cut one circle for the face and two circles for the body parts
B   Cut two circles for the remaining body parts

METHOD

Machine   Fused

▸ page 26

Satin stitch the head and tail parts. Sew a decorative machine stitch in circles on the shell. Embroider the antennae, and add a French knot as the eye.

Additional materials
Stitch a small bead onto the end of each antenna.

METHOD

Machine   Fused

▸ page 26

Use satin stitches and blanket stitches on the circles. Stitch two curved lines as antennae.

Additional materials
Glue on wobbly eyes to give the caterpillar an inquisitive look.

Tip
If you intend this motif for a baby or young child, make sure you leave off the antennae beads as these could be a choking hazard.

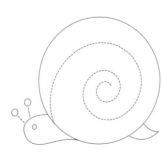

64 PRICKLY PORCUPINE

65 FRIENDLY FROG

This one-piece easy-to-make porcupine is decorated with embroidered straight stitches, splashed as spines over the back of his body.

This big, goggle-eyed frog will make you smile—go on, give him a home in one of your projects!

A

A   **B**

A   Cut one porcupine shape

A   Cut one face, one body, and two legs
B   Cut two round eyes

METHOD

Machine   Freezer
              paper

▸ page 28

Apply the shape using the freezer paper technique. Embroider a curved line to indicate the porcupine's nose and straight lines for the spikes.

Additional materials
Add a button as an eye.

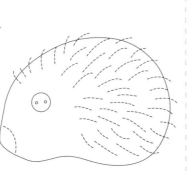

METHOD

Machine   Fused

▸ page 26

Decorate all edges with blanket stitch. Embroider the mouth with double lines of backstitch.

Additional materials
Glue on two wobbly eyes.

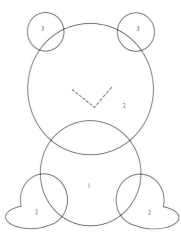

66 WINKING KITTY

What is sweeter than a kitten? A winking kitten! Appliqué one wide-open eye on the cat's face and embroider the other in a "V" wink shape.

A   **B**   **C**

A Cut one face
B Cut three stripes and a round eye shape
C Cut two ears and two paws

METHOD

Machine   Freezer paper

▸ page 28

Embroider the winking eye and nose on the round face shape. Use the freezer paper appliqué technique for the kitty's face and fuse all other parts. For added definition, the ears and paws are finished with satin stitch.

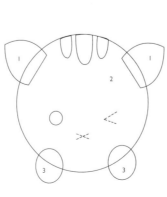

67 WIDE-EYED OWL

This perching owl is put together from easy-to-cut shapes, and provides a great opportunity to use up scraps of different patterned fabrics from your stash.

A   **B**   **C**   **D**   **E**

A Cut one face
B Cut one perch shape
C Cut two eye patches
D Cut two wings and two inner eyes
E Cut two ears and a beak

METHOD

Machine   Fused

▸ page 26

Finish the body with a cross stitch or the stitch of your choice. All other parts are stitched with blanket stitch.

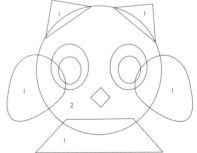

> **Tip**
> To save time, cut the owl body and perch shape from one piece of fabric. Turn back to the mix and match panel on page 91 for an example of this method.

68 MOONFACE PUPPY

The puffy appliqué technique adds dimension to this adorable puppy dog, which is easy to make with great results.

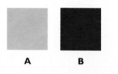

A   **B**

A   Cut two circles for the face
B   Cut two ears

METHOD

Machine   3D

▶ page 34

Follow the instructions on pages 34–35. Use fabric glue to attach the ears. Embroider the mouth.

Additional materials
Glue on two wobbly eyes for a fun effect.

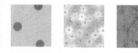

Tips
If you have accidentally stitched all round the face before adding the filling, slit a small hole on the back and stuff with fiberfill. Be careful not to slit the front fabric! Close the slit with a slipstitch.

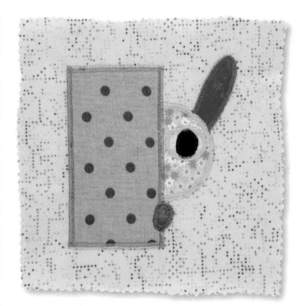

69 PEEK-A-BOO

This whimsical appliqué will brighten any project and it's easily adaptable—for variation, try using one of the doll figures, or another animal from this section, instead of a bunny.

A   **B**   **C**   **D**   **E**

A   Cut one rectangle
B   Cut one face

C   Cut one long ear and one paw
D   Cut one eye shape
E   Cut one eye pupil

METHOD

Machine   Fused

▶ page 26

Satin stitch all edges.

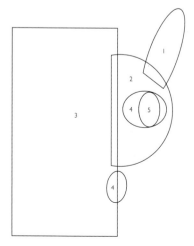

70 HIDE AND SEEK SURPRISE

Wouldn't this tiny mouse look gorgeous popping out from a pocket on a pair of jeans or a bag?

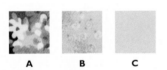

A   Cut one semicircle
B   Cut one semicircle for the face, two outer ear shapes and two paws
C   Cut two inner ear shapes and two eyes

METHOD

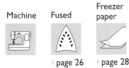

▸ page 26   ▸ page 28

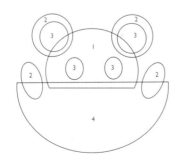

Start by fusing the parts of the mouse, working zigzag around all visible parts. Then use the freezer paper technique on the half circle.

Additional materials
Glue on two wobbly eyes.

71 BROWN BEAR

With his big face, round eyes, and pink nose, this cuddly bear is bound to charm. Experiment with plush fabrics to make him even more cuddly.

A   Cut two paws, one outer face, and two eyes
B   Cut one body, two ears, and one inner face

METHOD

▸ page 26

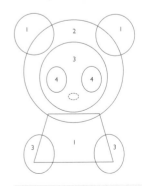

Fuse all parts and finish the edges with matching satin stitch. Embroider a small nose just under the bear's eyes.

Additional materials
Glue on two wobbly eyes. Use embellishment glue to attach a sparkly flower to the bear's belly.

Tip
Place the bear's body under any of the round-shaped animal faces for variation.

72 FUNNY BUNNY

This funny bunny, finished with a playful decorative stitch and embellished with two fabric flowers, is one of several animal faces based on the same round shape.

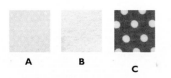

A   B   C

A   Cut one face
B   Cut two eyes
C   Cut four ears

METHOD

Machine   Fused   3D

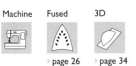

▸ page 26   ▸ page 34

See the three-dimensional appliqué technique on page 36 for how to fold the bunny's ears.

Additional materials
Stick on two wobbly eyes and two fabric flowers.

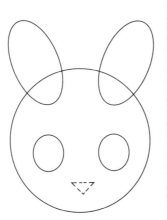

73 SO SOFT SHEEP

This sheep is made with fake fur fabric and is extra soft and cuddly. He'd be perfect on a bath robe, a towel, or even a sweatshirt or pinafore.

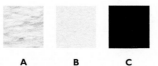

A   B   C

A   Cut one body
B   Cut one face and two legs
C   Cut two feet and two eyes

METHOD

Machine   Fused

▸ page 26

Fuse all parts of the sheep in place. Zigzag the edge of the fake fur fabric and use a straight stitch on the sheep's head. Embroider a triangular nose.

Tip
No special needle is required to sew fabrics like fake fur. It is wise to use a longer zigzag stitch so that you can carefully pull the hairs from under the threads with a needle. Alternatively, trim the fur on the edges with snippers before you sew.

74 REVERSE BABY ELEPHANT

A big friend for any project, small or large, this endearing baby elephant uses the reverse appliqué technique, fusing for the ear, and decorative machine stitching.

A   **B**

A Cut one piece large enough to cover the entire elephant shape

B Cut one ear

METHOD

Machine   Fused   Reverse

▸ page 26   ▸ page 32

Work straight stitch around the edges. Fuse on the ear and finish with a decorative machine satin stitch.

Additional materials
Glue on a wobbly eye.

75 CHEEKY SQUIRREL

This hungry squirrel has found an acorn to eat (find the acorn too on page 67). Add wobbly, bead, or button eyes if desired.

A   **B**   **C**   **D**   **E**

A Cut one body, one head, and one tail

B Cut one arm and two ears

C Cut two eyes and two feet

D Cut one acorn cup

E Cut one acorn

METHOD

Hand   Raw edge

▸ page 30

Work backstitch on all visible edges of the squirrel and acorn. Add the same stitching to the tail to indicate the curl.

76 LITTLE TAWNY OWL

Adorn your school books or journal with some added wisdom. This cute fused and machine sewn owl is surprisingly quick to sew.

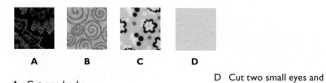

A   B   C   D

A Cut one body
B Cut one face
C Cut two wings and the bottom of the body

D Cut two small eyes and one beak

METHOD

Machine   Fused

▶ page 26

Finish by machining satin stitch on the wings, eyes, and beak. Edge all other parts with blanket stitch.

Use it here

73 + 75

TOTE BAGS

Appliqué cute animals onto plain tote bags to make pretty gifts. (These particular motifs can be found on pages 97 and 98.)

77 QUICK CHICKS

78 PUDGY PENGUIN

These two chicks are made from fused felt and decorated with ribbon. This appliqué is fast and easy to make.

Use black fabric for the body and wings of your penguin or, as in this example, use patterned black-and-white fabric to make your design more dynamic.

A   **B**   **C**

A Cut one cart shape and two inner eye circles
B Cut two bodies, two heads and three beak parts
C Cut two wheels and two outer eyes

A   **B**   **C**   **D**

A Cut one body and two wing shapes   **D** Cut one beak and two feet
B Cut one inner body shape
C Cut two eyes

METHOD

Fused

▸ page 26

Additional materials
Cut a piece of ribbon long enough to cover the length of the cart and glue it in place.

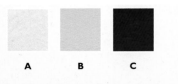

METHOD

Machine   **Fused**

▸ page 26

Fuse all parts, machine sew narrow zigzag stitch around the penguin's body, and satin stitch around the wings. Backstitch around the inner body and work one stitch on the beak.

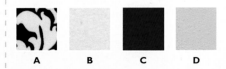

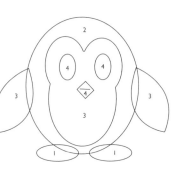

79 SLEEPY TEDDY

This cute, sleepy-looking teddy face is finished with satin stitches all around and simple embroidery stitches. It would work especially well on blankets and nightwear.

A   **B**

A   Cut one face shape
B   Cut one top of head

METHOD

Machine   Fused

▸ page 26

Fuse both parts of the motif and finish the edges with satin stitch. Work small hand stitches to indicate the eyes and mouth.

Additional materials
Glue on the two fabric bows.

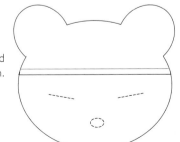

Use it here

76 + 77

BABY BIBS

Charming appliquéd animals work especially well on baby gifts and nursery presents. Here, baby bibs are decorated with an owl and chicks. (See pages 99 and 100 for these motifs.)

80 LONG-NECKED GIRAFFE | 81 SLEEPY TURTLE

This cute giraffe appliqué stands tall and proud, and is fast and easy to make. Try mixing this design with the tree motifs on page 68 to create a fitting environment for your giraffe to feed and live.

Decorative embroidery stitching outlines this sleepy turtle's body, and a machine-worked satin stitch is sewn around the shell shape.

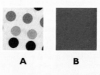

A   Cut one giraffe shape
B   Cut one ear

A   Cut one shell shape
B   Cut one body

METHOD

Hand   Fused

▶ page 26

Fuse and stitch the body first, then fuse the ear in place. Use a whipped backstitch on the edges of part A. Embroider the horn and top with 3 or 4 French knots grouped together. Work a whipped backstitch in a curved line for the giraffe's tail. Finish by embroidering the eye.

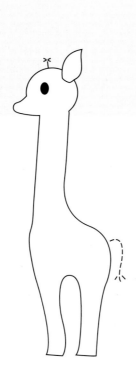

METHOD

Machine   Hand   Fused

▶ page 26

Mix machine stitching and hand embroidery. Start by fusing both A and B onto the base fabric. Apply a satin stitch around the edges of the shell. The body outline is finished with a whipped running stitch (see page 41). Embroider the eye using a regular backstitch.

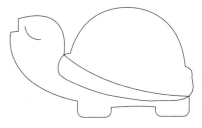

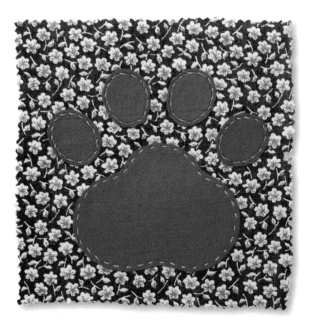

82 PAW PRINT

This paw print motif is used in the technique section to teach the fused appliqué technique (page 26–27). These simple shapes are a great opportunity for you to practice different machine and hand stitches.

A

A   Cut out center paw shape
    and four toes

METHOD

Hand   Raw edge

page 30

Work straight stitch around the edge of the center paw shape. Use a whipped running stitch around the edges of the toes.

Mix and Match

70 + 77

BIRD GARDEN

Use the template from motif 70 to fashion a semicircular bird's nest, and pop a chick or two from page 100 inside. The bird in flight uses the layered appliqué technique, which you will find on pages 24–25.

68 + 97

SUNDAE SURPRISE

Simple circle shapes can be turned into anything: animal faces, ice cream, or both! Use wobbly eyes for a playful effect that will suit a greeting card or journal cover.

MOTIFS 83–103

ALL THINGS GOOD TO EAT AND DRINK

Breakfast, fresh fruit, sushi, cakes, and candy—getting hungry? The following motifs will whet your appetite. Use these delicious food and drink motifs on your picnic hamper, or embellish your lunch bag. Work your favorite ice cream onto your placemat and dig in to an instant dessert!

83 JUICY FRUIT

Just one look at this juicy slice of lemon will have you reaching for the cooler. Change the colors and make yourself some orange, lime, or grapefruit slices too.

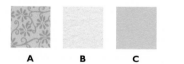

A   **B**   **C**

A Cut one large semicircle
B Cut one small semicircle
C Cut three lemon segments

METHOD

Hand   Machine   Freezer paper

▸ page 28

Use the freezer paper technique to attach the largest semicircle to the base fabric. Hand sew the three segments on the small semicircle and glue onto the large semicircle.

84 POLKADOT POPSICLE

This strawberry-flavored popsicle would look great on a cooler bag, or on items for the kitchen, picnics, or outdoor eating.

A   **B**

A Cut one popsicle
B Cut one stick shape

METHOD

Machine   Fused   Freezer paper

▸ page 26   ▸ page 28

Work satin stitch around the edge of the stick.

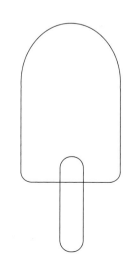

85 SET THE TABLE

86 BIRTHDAY TREAT

Reversed shapes of a fork and a spoon work well on a tablecloth or fabric placemat. Use easy-clean vinyl for tableware.

Celebrate with this colorful birthday pie appliqué, worked in a combination of freezer paper and fused appliqué with ribbon and sequin embellishments.

A

A   **B**

A   Cut one piece of fabric large enough to cover both motifs

A   Cut one pie and three flames
B   Cut three rectangles for the candles

METHOD

Machine   Reverse

▶ page 32

Work a decorative triple straight stitch around the edges.

METHOD

Machine   Fused   Freezer paper

▶ page 26   ▶ page 28

Use freezer paper to attach the pie and fuse the candles and flames. Sew a narrow zigzag stitch to indicate a border between the top and side of the pie.

Additional materials
Glue rickrack trim to the side of the pie. Sew a line of sequins, a bead in each, to the top.

87 SUSHI SNACK

Spice up a project with a simple serving of sushi. This example is cut from felt and outlined in satin stitch.

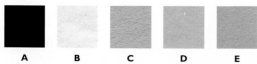

A Cut one outside shape (nori)
B Cut one circle (sushi rice)
C Cut one inner segment
D Cut one inner segment
E Cut one inner segment

METHOD

▸ page 26

Choose suitable fabric colors. Fuse and satin stitch all parts.

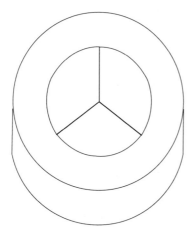

88 SWEET CANDY TREAT

These candy templates are cut with pinking shears to create an attractive edging, and are great gifts for friends and family.

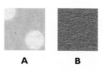

A Cut one candy shape
B Cut one candy shape

METHOD

▸ page 30

Cut the pieces with pinking shears. Sew a straight stitch just inside the edges of the candy.

89 BUTTON BERRY

The three-dimensional quality of these red, pink, and purple buttons look good enough to eat and the concentration of buttons provides impact and texture.

A | B

A Cut one berry shape
B Cut the sepals/stalk

METHOD

Machine Fused

▸ page 26

Finish all edges with satin stitch.

Additional materials
Sort through your red, pink and purple buttons to find ones that go together and glue into place.

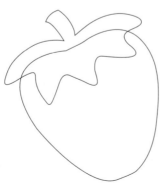

90 AN APPLE A DAY

This stylish appliqué motif uses a combination of freezer paper and fused appliqué techniques.

A | B | C

A Cut one apple
B Cut one half apple segment
C Cut one apple stalk and three pips

METHOD

Machine   Fused   Freezer paper

▸ page 26   ▸ page 28

Fuse the stalk onto the apple. Next, use the freezer paper technique on both the outside and inside apple shapes. Finish by fusing the three pips in place.

Tip
Turn your apple into a pair of cherries! Use the basic apple shape, cut it out twice, put the shapes next to each other, and add a stem and leaf (see the Revamped Gingham Purse on page 122).

91 PERFECT PEAR

92 WATERMELON WEDGE

This curvy, smooth, and easy-to-fuse pear would look super on a napkin or tablecloth.

Try combining this juicy slice of watermelon with the pear (motif 91) and apple (motif 90) on one single item, or make a set of funky fruity home accents for your kitchen.

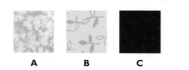

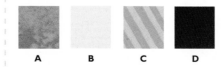

A Cut one pear
B Cut one inner section
C Cut one stalk and two pips

A Cut one small melon slice
B Cut one medium melon slice
C Cut one large melon slice

D Cut three pips

METHOD

Fused

▶ page 26

Fuse all pear pieces in place.

METHOD

Machine   Fused   Freezer paper

 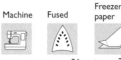

▶ page 26   ▶ page 28

Use the freezer paper technique on the three melon shapes and fuse the pips on the top melon portion.

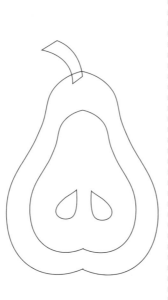

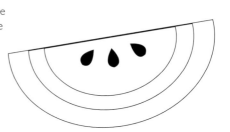

> ### Tip
> Dark colored backgrounds can overwhelm lighter colored materials. To prevent this, fuse an extra layer of interfacing to the back of the lighter fabric before applying it.

93 CUPCAKE DELIGHT

94 SWEET TOOTH

Add decorative embellishments to suit your celebration theme, then go ahead, blow out the candle. This sweet design will be an everlasting memento.

This colorful cake is decorated with sprinkles made from buttons. If you haven't got buttons, use beads instead.

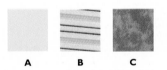

A   **B**   **C**

A   Cut one cupcake base
B   Cut one cupcake frosting
C   Cut one candle and one flame

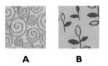

A   **B**

A   Cut one cupcake base
B   Cut one cupcake frosting

METHOD

Machine   Fused

▸ page 26

Use satin stitch in matching colors on all parts. Embroider five backstitch lines on the bottom of the cupcake for its contours.

Additional materials

Glue on one fabric flower and add a button to its center.

METHOD

Machine   Fused

▸ page 26

Finish the edges with a decorative over-edge stitch.

Additional materials

Sprinkle buttons on the frosting and hand sew in place using clear thread.

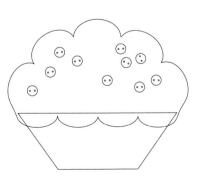

95 COTTON CANDY

Cotton candy or ice cream? You can have either with this clever motif. Let it be what you want it to be, and enjoy—it's calorie-free after all.

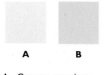

A   **B**

A Cut one cone/cup
B Cut one filling

METHOD

Hand   Machine

Sew satin stitch on the cone and work blanket stitch by hand on the filling. Sew three backstitch embroidery lines on the cone to indicate its shape.

96 ICE CREAM DREAM

The dream of every ice cream lover, this huge bowl is filled with fused scoops in a variety of colors, or flavors. Go on, indulge yourself!

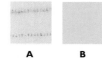

A   **B**   **C**   **D**

A Cut one bowl   D Cut one scoop
B Cut one scoop of ice cream   of ice cream
C Cut one scoop of ice cream

METHOD

Machine   Fused

▸ page 26

Choose matching colored threads to satin stitch all edges.

Additional materials
If desired, glue on sparkly embellishments or button sprinkles.

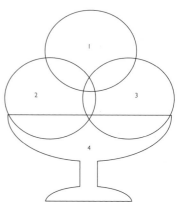

97 TWICE AS NICE

98 TIME FOR TEA

Two scoops are twice as nice as one, so treat yourself to this tasty duo. Covered with sequin sprinkles that shine and catch the eye, this ice cream cone is bound to satisfy.

This cherry teapot is padded for extra dimension. Why not mix and match with the teacup to your right, and create a neat set of tea cozies for your guests?

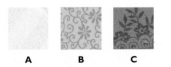

A   Cut one triangular cone
B   Cut one scoop of ice cream
C   Cut one scoop of ice cream

A   Cut one teapot

METHOD

METHOD

▸ page 26

▸ page 34

Blanket stitch all around. Embroider three backstitch lines on the cone.

Satin stitch all around the edges and along the design lines.

Additional materials
Sew on colorful sequins with beads at the center, freely arranged on one of the scoops.

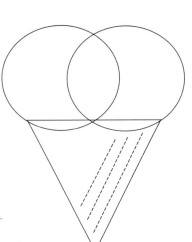

99 PATTERNED TEACUP

100 SHAKEN NOT STIRRED

Add the cupcakes (motifs 93 and 94) to this elegant teacup design and fuse to your coasters to make teatime a real indulgence.

How do you take yours? Change the color of the drink to match your favorite tipple. If your drink is sparkling, add a few sequin bubbles.

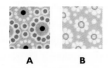

A   B

A   Cut one semicircle for the cup
B   Cut one cup base and one handle

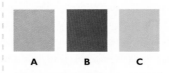

A   B   C

A   Cut one cocktail glass
B   Cut one oval for the drink
C   Cut one orange slice

METHOD

Machine   Fused

▸ page 26

Additional materials
Cut a length of decorative ribbon to fit across the cup and fuse in place.

METHOD

Fused

▸ page 26

Fuse all parts and sew a satin stitch line to indicate the edge of the glass.

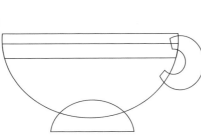

101 TASTY TOAST

102 SUNNY SIDE UP

Brown and off-white fabrics combine to make this great design. Use as part of a larger breakfast arrangement (see the mix and match variation, on your right).

No breakfast is complete without the perfect egg. Use yellow or orange and white felt for the egg motif, and experiment with complementary colors and patterned fabrics for the plate.

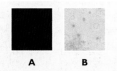

A   **B**

A   Cut one outer crust shape
B   Cut one center section

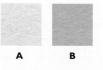

A   **B**

A   Cut one egg white shape
B   Cut one plate and one egg yoke

METHOD

Machine   Fused

▸ page 26

Use matching threads to satin stitch around the crust and work blanket stitch on the inner bread shape.

METHOD

Machine   Fused

▸ page 26

Work satin stitch on the plate and egg yoke, and sew blanket stitch around the egg white.

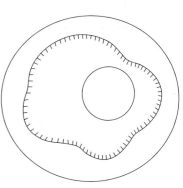

Mix and Match

101 + 102

BREAKFAST PLATE

Combine the toast and egg to your left on one plate for a delicious breakfast.

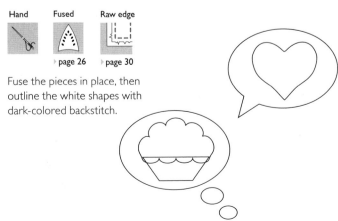

94 + 96

PERFECT PUDDING

Mix the cupcake frosting from motif 94 with the ice cream bowl from motif 96 to make a spectacular pudding. A handful of stick-on gems make this a real treat.

---

103 IN YOUR DREAMS

Dreaming of candy? Appliqué a cartoon balloon in white fabric and emphasize the edges with dark backstitch to express what's in your dreams.

A	B	C

A   Cut one speech balloon, one large oval, and two small ovals
B   Cut one heart and one cupcake frosting
C   Cut one cupcake base

METHOD

Hand	Fused	Raw edge
	▶ page 26	▶ page 30

Fuse the pieces in place, then outline the white shapes with dark-colored backstitch.

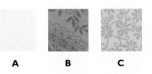

CHAPTER FOUR

Now that you have designed and created your appliqué patterns, you may wish to apply them to a larger project. The following pages demonstrate how, using four super examples. Find out how to personalize your journal, adorn a plain T-shirt or top with a cute kitty or squirrel, or fasten a rosette to a hat, clutch, or shoe. All projects are complete with step-by-step instruction, and photography of the finished result.

PROJECTS

JOURNALS

GLAMOR GIRL

If you want to make a journal cover with stitched appliqué, you'll have to work the appliqué pattern first, and then stick the cover to the journal. See page 119 to find out how.

WANT MORE?

This young lady could be holding hands with a boy, such as Baseball Buddy (page 76), for the cover of a friendship journal.

SLEEEPING BEAUTY'S JOURNAL

Your journal is private and should be a reflection of you. Personalize it with your favorite appliqué motif. This one's for Sleeping Beauty.

WANT MORE?

What is Sleeping Beauty dreaming of? Add a speech bubble (page 115) and an image of her thoughts.

METHOD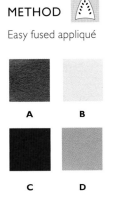

Easy fused appliqué

A	**B**
C	**D**

A Cut one egg shape
B Cut one face
C Cut the hair
D Cut two hands

MATERIALS

- Hardcover journal
- Fabric (enough to cover the outside of the journal when open, plus 1 in. (2.5 cm) all the way around)
- Appliqué fabrics
- Lace or ribbon trim
- Fabric flower
- Small gem or button

Get the template
Sleeping Beauty
on page 81

METHOD

Fused and hand stitched appliqué

A	**B**
C	

A Cut all body parts: face, neck, arms, and legs (Pretty Red Dress)
B Cut the hair (Dancing with Butterflies)
C Cut one dress (Dancing with Butterflies)

MATERIALS

- Hardcover journal
- Fabric (enough to cover the outside of the journal when open, plus 1 in. (2.5 cm) all the way around)
- Appliqué fabrics
- Lace or ribbon trim
- Flower eyelets or other embellishments
- Five small gems

Get the template
Pretty Red Dress
on page 76
Dancing with Butterflies
on page 77

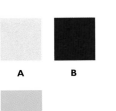

PUTTING IT ALL TOGETHER

1 Iron the fabric to avoid any undesired creases.
2 Open up your journal and lay it on the main fabric. Cut the fabric 1 in. (2.5 cm) outside the journal. Clip off the corners of the fabric.
3 Place the fabric wrong side up and the journal open in the middle.
4 Move the papers out of the way and fold over one side of the fabric to the inside of the cover and glue it in place. Repeat on the other side. Don't pull the fabric too tight—you need enough ease to be able to close the book.
5 Hold up the pages in the center, and cut out a little notch of fabric at the top spine, leaving about ¼ in. (6 mm) extra fabric past the edge of the journal. Don't cut all the way to the spine. Do the same at the bottom of the spine.
6 Glue down the short edges of the fabric, top and bottom, as you did the long sides in step 4.
7 Embroider the eyes and mouth on the face and then fuse the appliqué shapes in place on the front of the journal.
8 Stick on the fabric flower and stick a gem in the center.
9 Glue on lace or ribbon for extra embellishment.

PUTTING IT ALL TOGETHER

1 Iron the fabric to avoid any undesired creases.
2 Open your journal and lay it on the main fabric. Cut the fabric 1 in. (2.5 cm) outside the journal. Clip off the corners of the fabric.
3 Work out where the front of the journal will be on the fabric—use a chalk pencil to mark it, if desired. Embroider the eyes and mouth on the face appliqué and then fuse the appliqué shapes in place on the base fabric. Backstitch around the edge of the dress.
4 Stick on the gems to make a flower in the girl's hair. Stick on the ribbon and add eyelet flowers or other decorations.
5 Place the fabric wrong side up and the journal open in the middle.
6 Move the papers out of the way and fold over one side of the fabric to the inside of the cover and glue in place. Repeat on the other side. Don't pull the fabric too tight—you need enough ease to be able to close the book.
7 Hold up the pages in the center, and cut out a little notch of fabric at the top spine, leaving about ¼ in. (6 mm) extra fabric past the edge of the journal. Don't cut all the way to the spine. Do the same at the bottom of the spine.
8 Glue down the short edges of the fabric, top and bottom, as you did the long sides in step 6.

TOPS

TOP CAT

Adorn a top with this cute kitty cat. Choose a complementary color for your appliqué and choose threads to go with your shirt.

WANT MORE?

Use fusible interfacing on the inside of the shirt underneath your appliqué to help prevent distortion while sewing, and the shirt from stretching too much in that area.

SQUIRREL ON YOUR SHIRT

Adorn a plain shirt with an inquisitive squirrel. Choose a green shirt to accentuate the natural, earthy colors. He likes acorns, but you could also feed him a cute cupcake by mixing and matching with the red shirt design below.

WANT MORE?

If the squirrel looks hungry, add some extra acorns to keep him happy. If you're making this shirt for a child, embroider the squirrel's eyes instead of using the fusible appliqué method.

WANT MORE?

Hold the cat template up to a window and trace it on the back to get a reversed cat. Then cut one cat and one reversed cat from the same fabric and add one to each back pocket of your jeans. Note that washing instructions for a garment may change after you have appliquéd it, due to the chosen material of the appliqué. Be safe and hand wash appliquéd clothing!

METHOD

Fused and hand stitched appliqué

A

A   Cut one cat

MATERIALS

- Store-bought top or shirt
- Appliqué fabric of your choice
- Fusible web
- Embroidery thread

Get the template
Kitty Cat on page 87

PUTTING IT ALL TOGETHER

1 Wash your shirt.

2 Trace the template of the Kitty Cat (page 87) and cut it out from your appliqué fabric.

3 Arrange the appliqué on the front of the shirt.

4 Using the fused appliqué method, secure the cat to the shirt.

5 Hand stitch blanket stitch all around the edge.

6 Press your appliqué to help the appliqué relax into place.

7 Using straight stitches, embroider three crosses on the cat's face to indicate the eyes and nose.

METHOD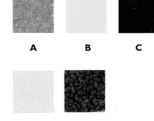

Fused appliqué with machine satin stitch edging

A   **B**   **C**

D   **E**

A   Cut one face, one body, and one tail shape.

B   Cut two ears and one tummy patch

C   Cut two eyes and two paws

D   Cut a semi-circle shape for the cup of the acorn

E   Cut a semi-circle shape for the nut

MATERIALS

- Fabric of your choice
- Store-bought T-shirt

Get the template
Cheeky Squirrel on page 98
Snacks for Squirrels on page 67

PUTTING IT ALL TOGETHER

1 Wash and iron the T-shirt.

2 Trace the template and cut out the pieces.

3 Arrange them on the shirt front.

4 Using the fused appliqué method, secure the pieces on the shirt.

5 Machine satin stitch around all the visible edges of the fabric pieces, except the eyes.

6 Add an extra bit of satin stitch to indicate the curl inside the squirrel's tail.

7 Using small backstitches, embroider the shape of the mouth onto the squirrel's face.

ACCESSORIES

CUTE CORSAGE
Add a three-dimensional flower to any of your accessories and let it bloom all year long. You'll need just two fabrics, one for the front and the other for the back.

REVAMPED GINGHAM PURSE
Scored a great but plain purse at the thrift store? Fabric scraps and ribbon-roses will turn it into a wonderful eye catcher you will be proud of.

METHOD

Easy fused appliqué.

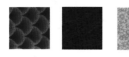

A	B	C

A Cut two cherries
   (or as many as needed)

B Cut two stems
   (or as many as needed)

C Cut one leaf
   (or as many as needed)

MATERIALS

- Store-bought clutch
- Fabrics of your choice
- Fusible web
- Ready-to-use
  ribbon roses

Get the template
This appliqué is based on
motif 90, which you will
find on page 108.

METHOD

Three-dimensional appliqué
Fusible appliqué

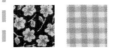

A	B

A Cut five petals (front)
B Cut five petals (back)

MATERIALS

- Front fabric
- Back fabric
- Fusible web
- One button

Get the template
Spring Crocus on page 70

PUTTING IT ALL TOGETHER

1 Cut the fabrics to the required shapes.

2 Lay the shapes and ready made roses on the purse in
combinations until you have an arrangement you like.

3 Following the method shown on pages 26–27, fuse the appliqué
shapes onto the purse in this order: start with the stem, then the
cherries, and add the leaf on top.

4 Arrange the flowers in a neat line to the right of the cherries to
balance the composition, and sew in place using several stitches.

PUTTING IT ALL TOGETHER

1 Cut the petals. Fuse each front petal to a back petal using
fusible web.

2 Decorate every petal with zigzag stitch inside the edges.

3 Hand sew running stitch through the bottom of every petal to
connect them. Draw the thread to overlap and gather the petals.
Knot the thread securely.

4 Sew the flower onto your project using several stitches and finish
by sewing on a center button.

WALL HANGINGS

JAPANESE-STYLE SOFT WALL HANGING
Fabric wall hangings add a very personal touch to your decor. Maybe it's time to consider using some fabric in your next decorating project? This piece has a distinctly Japanese flavor.

A BUG'S LIFE
Simple, bold images like this one are popular with children. This ladybug has been embellished with matching sequins. Enlarge the pattern pieces as desired before cutting out.

KOKESHI GIRL CANVAS
Apply scenery to a single motif design, and fuse to a canvas to create a composition that you can hang on your bedroom wall.

WANT MORE?
For a larger image, add a flower that the ladybug (below) could be visiting on its hunt for juicy aphids. Rather than edging the ladybug with sequins, use buttons for the dots on its wings and add a couple of wobbly eyes for fun.

WANT MORE?
For a large canvas design, appliqué extra trees and place the Kokeshi girl in a forest. Why not make her a friend to play with? You could even scale down the fruits and cakes on pages 105–115, and create a picnic scene, with woodland creatures, like an owl (page 94) or a squirrel (page 98).

METHOD

Fused appliqué

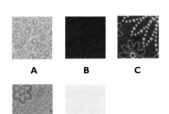

A   **B**   **C**

D   **E**

A   Cut one tree canopy
B   Cut one tree trunk
C   Cut one body, two sleeves
     and the hair
D   Cut one belt
E   Cut one face

MATERIALS

- Stretched art canvas
- Background fabric
- Appliqué fabrics
- Buttons for the tree
- One fabric flower
- Staple gun

Get the template
Button Tree on page 68
Creamy Kokeshi
on page 82

PUTTING IT ALL TOGETHER

1 Iron the fabric to avoid any undesired creases in the finished project.

2 Measure and cut your base fabric large enough to cover the entire canvas plus about 1–1½ in. (2.5–4 cm) of fabric to fold over the edges to the back.

3 Arrange the appliqué motifs on the base fabric and fuse them in place. Stitch around the edges as desired using machine stitches.

4 Arrange the buttons on the tree and the fabric flower on the girl. Sew and/or glue them on.

5 Lay the appliquéd base fabric wrong side up and position the canvas face down in the center of the fabric.

6 Fold the fabric around the canvas, as if wrapping a gift, pulling tight to prevent gapping. Use the staple gun to tack the fabric to the back of the wood frame. Start with the long sides and then do the same with the short sides. To finish the corners, fold and tuck in the overlap and staple it down.

METHOD

Fused appliqué

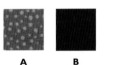

A   **B**

A   Cut one ladybug
B   Cut one ladybug head

MATERIALS

- Stretched art canvas
- Background fabric
- Red and green fabrics
- Sequins

Get the template
Lovely Ladybug
on page 91

PUTTING IT ALL TOGETHER

1 Iron the fabric to avoid any undesired creases in the finished project.

2 Measure and cut your base fabric large enough to cover the entire canvas plus about 1–1½ in. (2.5–4 cm) of fabric to fold over the edges to the back.

3 Arrange the ladybug body on the base fabric and fuse it in place. Position the head and fuse that in place too.

4 Stitch red and green sequins around the edge of the ladybug, overlapping them in a continuous line.

5 Embroider the line between the wing cases with backstitch and add cross stitches for the spots.

6 Lay the appliquéd base fabric wrong side up and position the canvas face down in the center of the fabric.

7 Fold the fabric around the canvas, as if wrapping a gift, pulling tight to prevent gapping. Use the staple gun to tack the fabric to the back of the wood frame. Start with the long sides and then do the same with the short sides. To finish the corners, fold and tuck in the overlap and staple down.

INDEX

WEB RESOURCES

The Internet is a wonderful source of information and there is plenty of appliqué inspiration to be found on the web. Download free patterns or look at other artist's creations to get ideas for your own projects. Many fabrics can, of course, be purchased at your local fabric store, but the Internet brings larger stores (that otherwise wouldn't be so accessible) to you. For starters, check out some of the weblinks below:

Manhattan Fabrics
www.manhattanfabrics.com
Tel: 212-944-7101
Exclusive designer fabrics from the world's most renowned designers.

Paron Fabrics
www.paronfabrics.com
Tel: 212-768-3266
Diverse and up-to-date inventory of (designer) fabrics and full lines of patterns.

j. caroline designs
www.jcarolinecreative.com
Tel: 866-522-7654
One-stop shopping for all your creative needs.

J & O Fabrics
www.jandofabrics.com
Tel: 856-663-2121
J & O Fabrics Center is the size of a supermarket! Online you'll find everything you need.

Duncan Enterprises
www.duncancrafts.com
Tel: 559-291-4444
Aleene's craft glues.

Pellon Products
www.shoppellon.com
Tel: 770-491-8001 (ext: 2980)
Shop here for craft materials like *Wonder Under*™ iron-on adhesive and interfacings.

CREDITS

All illustrations and photographs are the copyright of Quarto Publishing plc. While every effort has been made to credit contributors, Quarto would like to apologize should there have been any omissions or errors—and would be pleased to make the appropriate correction for future editions of the book.

Special thanks to Stephen Bogod at Bernina's for loan of the Bernina Activa 230PE sewing machine for photography:

Bernina Sewing Machines
50–52 Great Sutton Street
London EC1V 0DJ
Tel: (0044) 20 7549 7849
Web: www.bernina.co.uk
Email: info@bernina.co.uk

ACKNOWLEDGMENTS

The author would like to thank the wonderful people of Manhattan Fabrics and Paron Fabrics, j. caroline designs, Duncan Enterprises, Pellon, and J & O Fabrics for kindly supplying many of the fabrics and other materials used for the samples in this book.

She also wants to say a great thank you to the people at Quarto Publishing for all their support and for making this book possible.

Finally, a heartfelt thank you goes to the loving husband who endured a lot of appliqué talk and fabrics all around. Thank you for believing and encouraging.